Quick
BABY KNITS

Quick
BABY KNITS

OVER 25 DESIGNS FOR 0-3 YEAR OLDS

Debbie Bliss

ST. MARTIN'S GRIFFIN
New York

This book is for Will and Nell

QUICK BABY KNITS. Text and designs © Debbie Bliss 1999.
Photography copyright © Sandra Lousada 1999.
All rights reserved. Printed in Singapore.
No part of this book may be reproduced in any manner whatsoever
without written permission except in the case of brief quotations
embodied in critical articles or reviews.
For information, address St. Martin's Press, 175 Fifth Avenue, NY 10010.

Library of Congress Cataloguing-in-Publication Data available on request.

ISBN 0-312-20251-2

First St. Martin's Griffin edition: 1999

10 9 8 7 6 5 4 3 2 1

First published in the United Kingdom in 1999 by Ebury Press,
20 Vauxhall Bridge Road, London SW1V 2SA

Photography by Sandra Lousada
Designed by Alison Shackleton
Styling by Christine Knox
Pattern checking by Tina Egleton

Printed and bound in Singapore by Tien Wah Press

ALSO BY DEBBIE BLISS
Toy Knits
New Baby Knits
Kids' Country Knits
Baby Knits
Kids' Knits for Heads, Hands and Toes
Nursery Knits
Teddy Bears

CONTENTS

INTRODUCTION

There is still a tremendous amount of enthusiasm for knitting, particularly among those who love to see children wearing garments that have been handcrafted rather than mass produced, but who do not have the skill or the time to knit complicated designs. Baby gifts are also more special when they have been made rather than bought and simple garments or accessories are a perfect way for the less confident knitter to produce a lovingly crafted present.

Simple knits do not have to be boring or unexciting – lovely effects can be produced by using a beautiful, good quality yarn in a garter or moss stitch design, a classic style can be enhanced with colourful embroidery; and attractive colourwork can be achieved by using small, easy-to-follow patterns.

Quick Baby Knits is a collection of over 25 designs in which the message is less is more.

Debbie Bliss

Basic information

NOTES

Figures for larger sizes are given in round ( ) brackets. Where only one figure appears, this applies to all sizes. Work figures given in square [ ] brackets the number of times stated afterwards.

Where 0 appears, no stitches or rows are worked for this size.

The yarn amounts given in the instructions are based on average requirements and should therefore be considered approximate. If you want to use a substitute yarn, choose a yarn of the same type and weight as the one recommended. The following descriptions of the various Rowan or Jaeger yarns are meant as a guide to the yarn weight and type (ie, cotton, mohair, wool, etc.). Remember that the description of the yarn weight is only a rough guide and you should always test a yarn first to see if it will achieve the correct tension.

Magpie Aran: a fisherman medium-weight yarn (100% pure new wool); approximately 150m/164yd per 100g/3½oz hank.

Cotton Glacé: a lightweight cotton yarn (100% cotton); approximately 112m/123yd per 50g/1¾oz ball.

Designer DK: a double knitting-weight yarn (100% pure new wool); approximately 115m/125yd per 50g/1¾oz ball.

DK Handknit Cotton: a medium-weight cotton yarn (100% cotton); approximately 85m/90yd per 50g/1¾oz ball.

DK Tweed: a double knitting-weight yarn (100% pure new wool); approximately 110m/120yd per 50g/1¾oz ball.

Super Chunky Tweed: a chunky weight (100% wool); approximately 80m/88yd per 100g/3½ oz ball.

Cashmere 4 ply: a 4 ply yarn (90% Cashmere, 10% polyamide); approximately 98m/108yd per 25g/1 oz ball.

Pure Cotton: a double knitting-weight cotton yarn (100% cotton); approximately 112m/123yd per 50g/1¾ oz ball.

The amount of a substitute yarn needed is determined by the number of metres/yards needed rather than by the number of grams/ounces. If you are unsure when choosing a substitute, ask your yarn shop for advice.

TENSION

Each pattern in this book specifies a tension – the number of stitches and rows per centimetre/inch that should be obtained with the given needles, yarn and stitch pattern. Check your tension carefully before commencing work.

Use the same yarn, needles and stitch pattern as those to be used for the main work and knit a sample at least 12.5cm/5in square. Smooth out the finished sample on a flat surface, but do not stretch it. To check the tension, place a ruler horizontally on the sample and mark 10cm/4in across with pins. Count the number of stitches between the pins. To check the row tension, place a ruler vertically on the sample and mark 10cm/4in with pins. Count the number of rows between the pins. If the number of stitches and rows is greater than specified, try again using larger needles; if less, use smaller needles.

The stitch tension is the most important element to get right.

In the US, balls or hanks of yarn are sold in ounces, not in grams; the weights of the relevant Rowan or Jaegar yarns are given on this page.

STANDARD ABBREVIATIONS

A few specific knitting terms may be unfamiliar to some readers. The list below explains the abbreviations used in this book to help the reader understand how to follow the various stitches and stages.

alt = alternate
beg = begin(ning)
cont = continue

The following terms may be unfamiliar to US readers:

UK TERMS	US TERMS
Aran wool	'fisherman' (unbleached wool) yarn
ball band	yarn wrapper
cast off	bind off
DK wool	knitting worsted yarn
make up (garment)	finish (garment)
rib	ribbing
stocking stitch	stockinette stitch
tension	gauge

dec = decreas(e)ing
foll = following
inc = increas(e)ing
k = knit
m1 = make one by picking up the loop lying between st just worked and next st and working into the back of it
patt = pattern
p = purl
psso = pass slipped stitch over

rem = remain(ing)
rep = repeat
skpo = slip 1, knit 1, pass slipped stitch over
sl = slip
st(s) = stitch(es)
st st = stocking stitch
tbl = through back of loop
tog = together
yb = yarn back

yf = yarn forward
yon = yarn over needle
yrn = yarn round needle

IMPORTANT
Check on ball band for washing instructions. After washing, pat garment into shape and dry flat, away from direct heat.

BABY LAYETTE

MATERIALS

Jacket: 5(6:7) 50g balls of Rowan DK Handknit Cotton.
Pair each of 3¼mm (No 10/US 3), 3¾mm (No 9/US 4) and 4mm (No 8/US 6) knitting needles.
5(6:7) buttons.

Hat: 1(1:2) 50g balls of Rowan DK Handknit Cotton.
Pair of 4mm (No 8/US 6) knitting needles.

Blanket: Twelve 50g balls of Rowan DK Handknit Cotton.
Pair of 4mm (No 8/US 6) knitting needles.

TENSION

20 sts and 28 rows to 10cm/4in square over st st on 4mm (No 8/US 6) needles.

ABBREVIATIONS

See page 8.

JACKET
BACK

With 3¾mm (No 9/US 4) needles cast on 57(65:71) sts.
K 7 rows.
Change to 4mm (No 8/US 6) needles.
Beg with a k row, work in st st until Back measures 26(30:33)cm/10¼(11¾: 13)in from beg, ending with a p row.

Shape shoulders

Cast off 8(9:10) sts at beg of next 2 rows and 8(10:11) sts at beg of foll 2 rows. Leave rem 25(27:29) sts on a holder.

POCKET LININGS (MAKE 2)

With 4mm (No 8/US 6) needles cast on 15(17:20) sts. Beg with a k row, work 16(18:20) rows in st st. Leave these sts on a holder.

LEFT FRONT

With 3¾mm (No 9/US 4) needles cast on 33(37:40) sts.
K 7 rows.

Change to 4mm (No 8/US 6) needles.
1st row (right side) K.
2nd row K5, p to end.
Keeping the 5 sts at front edge in garter st (every row k) and remainder in st st, work a further 18(20:22) rows.

Place Pocket

Next row K6(7:7), sl next 15(17:20) sts onto a holder, k across sts of pocket lining, k to end.
Cont in st st with garter st border until Front measures 22(26:28)cm/8¾(10¼: 11)in from beg, ending at front edge.

Shape Neck

Next row Cast off 3, work 4(5:6) sts more, leave these 5(6:7) sts on a holder, work to end.
Dec one st at end of next row and cast off 2 sts at beg of foll row. Rep last 2 rows once more. Dec one st at neck edge on next 3 rows. 16(19:21) sts.
Work a few rows straight until Front matches Back to shoulder shaping, ending at side edge.

Shape Shoulder

Cast off 8(9:10) sts at beg of next row. Work 1 row. Cast off rem 8(10:11) sts.
Mark front edge to indicate buttons: first one to come just above the welt, last one 2 rows below neck shaping and rem 3(4:5) evenly spaced between.

RIGHT FRONT

With 3¾mm (No 9/US 4) needles cast on 33(37:40) sts.
K 7 rows.
Change to 4mm (No 8/US 6) needles.
Buttonhole row (right side) K1, k2tog, yf, k to end.
Next row P to last 5 sts, k5.
Next row K.
Keeping the 5 sts at front edge in garter st and remainder in st st, work a further 17(19:21) rows, making buttonhole as before to match markers on Left Front.

Place Pocket

Next row K12(13:13), sl next 15(17:20) sts onto a holder, k across sts of pocket lining, k to end.
Complete as given for Left Front, making buttonholes to match markers as before.

SLEEVES

With 4mm (No 8/US 6) needles cast on 32(36:42) sts.
K 10(14:18) rows.
Change to 3¾mm (No 9/US 4) needles.
K12(16:20) rows.
Change to 4mm (No 8/US 6) needles.
Beg with a k row, work in st st, inc one st at each end of every 3rd(3rd: 4th) row until there are 46(54:60) sts. Cont straight until sleeve measures 17(22:27) cm/6¾(8½:10¾)in from beg, ending with a p row. Cast off.

MEASUREMENTS

To fit age	3-6	6-9	9-12 months	
Jacket				
Actual chest measurement	59	67	73	cm
	23¼	26¼	28¾	in
Length	26	30	33	cm
	10¼	11¾	13	in
Sleeve seam	14	18	22	cm
(with cuff turned back)	5½	7	8¾	in
Blanket				
Approximately 76cm x 86cm/30in x 34in.				

COLLAR

Join shoulder seams.
With 3¼mm (No 10/US 3) needles and right side facing, slip the 5(6:7) sts from right front holder onto needle, join in yarn and k up 13(13:15) sts up right front neck, k back neck sts, dec 3 sts evenly, k up 13(13:15) sts down left front neck then k 5(6:7) sts from left front holder. 58(62:70) sts. K 10 rows.
Change to 4mm (No 8/US 6) needles. K 11 rows. Cast off knitwise.

POCKET TOPS

With 3¼mm (No 10/US 3) needles and right side facing, k across sts of pocket top. K 4 rows. Cast off knitwise.

TO MAKE UP

Catch down pocket linings and sides of pocket tops. Sew on sleeves, placing centre of sleeves to shoulders seams. Join side and sleeve seams, reversing seams half way on cuffs. Turn back cuffs. Sew on buttons.

HAT
TO MAKE

With 4mm (No 8/US 6) needles cast on 73(81:89) sts.
Work in garter st (every row k) for 13(15:18)cm/5(6:7)in.
Shape Top
Dec row K1, [k2tog, k6] to end.
K 1 row.
Dec row K1, [k2tog, k5] to end.

K 1 row.
Dec row K1, [k2tog, k4] to end.
Cont in this way, dec 9(10:11) sts on every alt row until 19(21:23) sts rem.
K 1 row.
Dec row K1, [k2tog] to end.
10(11:12) sts.
Break off yarn. Thread end through rem sts, pull up and secure. Join seam.

BLANKET
TO MAKE

With 4mm (No 8/US 6) needles cast on 151 sts.
Work in garter st (every row k) until blanket measures 86cm/34in from beg. Cast off.

EMBROIDERED JACKET AND SHOES

MATERIALS

Jacket: 4(5:6:7) 50g balls of Rowan DK Tweed.

Oddments of DK yarn in Green, Red and 2 shades of Pink for embroidery. Pair each of 3¼mm (No 10/US 3), 3¾mm (No 9/US 4) and 4mm (No 8/US 6) knitting needles.
5(6:7:8) buttons.

Shoes: One 50g ball of Rowan DK Tweed.

Oddments of DK yarn in Green, Red and 2 shades of Pink for embroidery. Pair of 3¾mm (No 9/US 4) knitting needles.

TENSION

21 sts and 36 rows to 10cm/4in square over moss st on 4mm (No 8/US 6) needles.

ABBREVIATIONS

See page 8.

JACKET
BACK

With 3¾mm (No 9/US 4) needles cast on 63(69:75:85) sts.
K 7 rows.
Change to 4mm (No 8/US 6) needles.
1st row K1, [p1, k1] to end.
This row forms moss st patt. Cont in moss st until work measures 25(30:35:39)cm/10(11¾:13¾:15½)in from beg.

Shape Shoulders

Cast off 10(11:12:14) sts at beg of next 2 rows and 9(10:11:13) sts at beg of foll 2 rows. Leave rem 25(27:29:31) sts on a holder.

POCKET LININGS (MAKE 2)

With 4mm (No 8/US 6) needles cast on 21(23:25:27) sts.
Work 32(34:36:38) rows in moss st as given for Back. Leave these sts on a holder.

MEASUREMENTS

Jacket					
To fit age	3-6	6-12	24	36 months	
Actual chest measurement	60	65	71	81	cm
	23½	25½	28	32	in
Length	25	30	35	39	cm
	10	11¾	13¾	15½	in
Sleeve seam	14	16	19	22	cm
(with cuff turned back)	5½	6¼	7½	8¾	in
Shoes	**0-6**	**6-12**	**12-18 months**		

LEFT FRONT

With 3¾mm (No 9/US 4) needles cast on 35(37:41:45) sts.
K 7 rows.
Change to 4mm (No 8/US 6) needles.
1st row (right side) [K1, p1] to last 5 sts, k5.
2nd row K5, [p1, k1] to end.

These 2 rows form moss st with 5 sts at front edge in garter st. Rep last 2 rows 14(15:16:17) times more, then work first row again.

Place Pocket

Next row K5, moss st 3(3:5:5), k next 21(23:25:27) sts, moss st to end.
Next row Moss st 6(6:6:8),

k21(23:25:27), moss st 3(3:5:5), k5.

Next row K5, moss st 3(3:5:5), cast off knitwise next 21(23:25:27) sts, moss st to end.

Next row Moss st 6(6:6:8), moss st across sts of pocket lining, moss st 3(3:5:5), k5.

Cont until Front measures 21(26:30:34)cm/8½(10¼:11¾:13½)in from beg, ending at front edge.

Shape Neck

Next row Cast off 3, patt 4(5:6:7) sts more; leave these 5(6:7:8) sts on a holder; patt to end.

Dec one st at neck edge on every row until 19(21:23:27) sts rem. Cont straight until Front measures same as Back to shoulder shaping, ending at side edge.

Shape Shoulder

Cast off 10(11:12:14) sts at beg of next row. Work 1 row. Cast off rem 9(10:11:13) sts.

Mark front edge to indicate buttons: first one on 4th row of welt, last one 2 rows below neck shaping and rem 3(4:5:6) evenly spaced between.

RIGHT FRONT

With 3¾mm (No 9/US 4) needles cast on 35(37:41:45) sts.

K 3 rows.

Buttonhole row (right side) K3, yf, k2tog, patt to end.

K 3 rows.

Change to 4mm (No 8/US 6) needles.

1st row (right side) K5, [p1, k1] to end.

2nd row [K1, p1] to last 5 sts, k5. These 2 rows form moss st with 5 sts at front edge in garter st. Rep these 2 rows 14(15:16:17) times more, then work first row again, making buttonholes to match markers on Left Front as before.

Place Pocket

Next row Moss st 6(6:6:8), k next 21(23:25:27), moss st 3(3:5:5), k5.

Next row K5, moss st 3(3:5:5), k21(23:25:27), moss st 6(6:6:8).

Next row Moss st 6(6:6:8), cast off

knitwise next 21(23:25:27) sts, moss st to last 5 sts, k5.

Next row K5, moss st 3(3:5:5), moss st across sts of pocket lining, moss st to end.

Complete as given for Left Front, making buttonholes to match markers as before.

SLEEVES

With 4mm (No 8/US 6) needles cast on 35(37:39:41) sts.

K 3 rows. Work 9 rows in moss st as given for Back. K 3 rows.

Change to 3¾mm (No 9/US 4) needles.

Work 14 rows in moss st.

Change to 4mm (No 8/US 6) needles. Cont in moss st, inc one st at each end of 3rd row and every foll 3rd(4th:4th:5th) row until there are 51(55:59:63) sts, working inc sts into moss st. Cont straight until sleeve measures 19(21:24:27)cm/7½(8¼:9½: 10¾)in from beg. Cast off.

COLLAR

Join shoulder seams.

With 3¼mm (No 10/US 3) needles and right side facing, slip 5(6:7:8) sts from right front holder onto needle, k up 17(17:19:19) sts up right front neck, k across back neck sts dec 4 sts evenly, k up 17(17:19:19) sts down left front neck, k across sts on left front holder. 65(69:77:81) sts.

1st row K3, p1, [k1, p1] to last 3 sts, k3.

Rep last row 7 times more.

Change to 4mm (No 8/US 6) needles. Work 10 rows as before. K 3 rows. Cast off loosely knitwise.

TO MAKE UP

Catch down pocket linings. Sew on sleeves, placing centre of sleeves to shoulder seams. Join side and sleeve seams, reversing seams on cuffs. Turn back cuffs. Sew on buttons. Embroider flowers below pocket tops and on

collar in satin stitch using darker shade of Pink and Red alternately with lighter shade of Pink at centres. With Green, embroider stems around flowers with stem stitch and leaves with lazy daisy stitch.

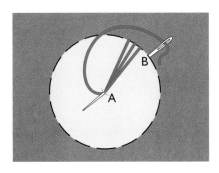

Satin Stitch

Bring needle out of A. Insert at B and emerge at A ready for next stitch.

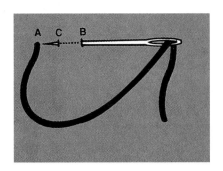

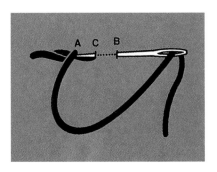

Stem Stitch

Bring needle out of A. Insert at B and emerge at C (half way).

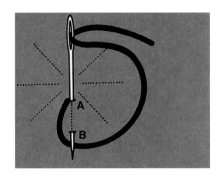

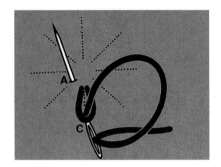

Lazy Daisy Stitch

Bring needle out at A. Insert back at A and emerge at B, looping yarn under the tip of needle. Pull needle through and over loop and insert at C. Emerge at A for next chain stitch.

SHOES
TO MAKE
With 3¾mm (No 9/US 4) needles cast on 30(33:36) sts.
K 31 rows.
Shape Instep
Next row K20(22:24), turn.
Next row K10(11:12), turn.
Work on this set of sts only for instep.
Next row (right side) K0(1:0), [p1, k1] to end.
Next row [K1, p1] to last 0(1:0) st, k0(1:0).
Rep last 2 rows 9(10:11) times more. Break off yarn.
With right side facing, rejoin yarn at base of instep and k up10(11:12) sts along side edge of instep, k across 10(11:12) sts of instep, k up 10(11:12) sts along other side of instep, k rem 10(11:12) sts. 50(55:60) sts. K 6 rows.
Next row (wrong side) [Pick up st 5 rows below, corresponding with next st on left-hand needle and k them tog] to end.
K 8(10:12) rows. Break off yarn.

Shape Sole
Next row With right side facing, sl first 20(22:24) sts onto right-hand needle, rejoin yarn and k10(11:12), turn.
Next row K9(10:11), k2tog, turn.
Rep last row 39(43:47) times more.
Next row K0(1:0), [k2tog] to end.
5(6:6) sts. Cast off. Join back seam, reversing seam on top 3cm/1¼in for cuff. Turn back cuff. Embroider flower at centre of instep in darker shade of Pink with lighter shade of Pink at centre and with Red, embroider buds at each side of flower. With Green, embroider stems with stem stitch and leaves with lazy daisy stitch.
Make one more.

BALLERINA TOP

MATERIALS
5(6:7) 50g balls of Rowan Cotton Glace.
Pair each of 2¾mm (No 12/US 2) and 3¼mm (No 10/US 3) knitting needles.

TENSION
25 sts and 34 rows to 10cm/4in square over st st on 3¼mm (No 10/US 3) needles.

ABBREVIATIONS
See page 8.

BACK
With 2¾mm (No 12/US 2) needles cast on 74(82:92) sts.

MEASUREMENTS

To fit age	6-12	12-18	24-36 months	
Actual chest measurement	59	65	73	cm
	23¼	25½	28¾	in
Length	23	26	32	cm
	9	10¼	12½	in
Sleeve seam	19	22	24	cm
	7½	8¾	9½	in

K 9 rows.
Change to 3¼mm (No 10/US 3) needles.
Beg with a k row, work 74(84:104) rows in st st.
Shape Shoulders
Cast off 10(11:12) sts at beg of next 4 rows. Cast off rem 34(38:44) sts.

LEFT FRONT
With 2¾mm (No 12/US 2) needles cast on 74(82:92) sts.
K 9 rows.
Change to 3¼mm (No 10/US 3) needles.
1st row (right side) K.

2nd row K4, p to end.

Rep last 2 rows 5(6:9) times more, then work the 1st row again.

Shape Neck

Next 2 rows K1, sl 1, yf, turn, sl 1, k1.

Next 2 rows K2, sl 1, yf, turn, sl 1, k2.

Next 2 rows K3, sl 1, yf, turn, sl 1, k3.

Next 2 rows K2, sl 1, yf, turn, sl 1, k2.

Next 2 rows K1, sl 1, yf, turn, sl 1, k1.

Next row K4 and slip these 4 sts onto safety pin, p to end.

Next row K to last 3 sts, k2tog, k1.

Next row P1, p2tog, p to end.

Rep last 2 rows until 32(36:42) sts rem, ending with a p row. Mark front edge of last row. Cont to dec at neck edge as before until 20(22:24) sts rem. Work 10(12:18) rows straight.

Shape Shoulder

Cast off 10(11:12) sts at beg of next row. Work 1 row. Cast off rem 10(11:12) sts.

RIGHT FRONT

With 2¾mm (No 12/US 2) needles cast on 74(82:92) sts.

K 9 rows.

Change to 3¼mm (No 10/US 3) needles.

1st row (right side) K.

2nd row P to last 4 sts, k4.

Rep last 2 rows 6(7:10) times more.

Shape Neck

Next 2 rows K1, sl 1, yf, turn, sl 1, k1.

Next 2 rows K2, sl 1, yf, turn, sl 1, k2.

Next 2 rows K3, sl 1, yf, turn, sl 1, k3.

Next 2 rows K2, sl 1, yf, turn, sl 1, k2.

Next 2 rows K1, sl 1, yf, turn, sl 1, k1.

Next row K4 and slip these 4 sts onto safety pin, k1, skpo, k to end.

Next row P to last 3 sts, p2tog tbl, p1.

Next row K1, skpo, k to end.

Rep last 2 rows until 32(36:42) sts rem, ending with a p row. Mark front edge of last row. Cont to dec at neck edge as before until 20(22:24) sts rem. Work 11(13:19) rows straight.

Shape Shoulder

Cast off 10(11:12) sts at beg of next row. Work 1 row. Cast off rem 10(11:12) sts.

SLEEVES

With 2¾mm (No 12/US 2) needles cast on 41(45:49) sts.

K 9 rows.

Change to 3¼mm (No 10/US 3) needles.

Beg with a k row, work 2 rows in st st.

Inc row K1, k twice in next st, k to last 3 sts, k twice in next st, k2.

Work 3 rows straight. Rep last 4 rows 13(14:15) times more. 69(75:81) sts. Work 0(6:8) rows straight. Cast off.

RIGHT NECK BAND AND COLLAR

With 2¾mm (No 12/US 2) needles, rejoin yarn at inside edge to the 4 sts on right front safety pin, k to end. Cont in garter st (every row k) until band fits along neck edge to marker.

Shape Collar

Inc one st at inside edge on next row and every foll alt row until there are 21 sts. Cont straight until collar fits along neck edge from marker to shoulder, ending at outside edge.

Next 2 rows K12, sl 1, yf, turn, sl 1, k 12.

Work 6 rows across all sts. Rep these 8 rows 4(5:6) times more, then work the 2 turning rows again. Work 6 rows across all sts. Cast off.

LEFT NECK BAND AND COLLAR

Work as given for Right Neck Band and Collar.

TIES (MAKE 2)

With 2¾mm (No 12/US 2) needles cast on 5 sts.

Work in garter st until tie measures approximately 36(41:46)cm/14(16: 18) in. Cast off.

TO MAKE UP

Join shoulder seams and back seam of collar. Sew bands and collar in position. Attach one end of ties to turning rows of neck shaping at fronts. Sew on sleeves, placing centre of sleeves to shoulder seams. Join side and sleeve seams, leaving an opening at right side seam for tie.

PARKA

MATERIALS

Five 100g hanks of Rowan Magpie. Pair each of 3¼mm (No 9/US 4) and 4½mm (No 7/US 7) knitting needles. 10 buttons.

ABBREVIATIONS

See page 8.

MEASUREMENTS

To fit age		2-3 years
Actual chest measurement	88 cm	34½ in
Length	43 cm	17 in
Sleeve seam	24 cm	9½ in

TENSION

18 sts and 26 rows to 10cm/4in square over st st on 4½mm (No 7/US 7) needles.

BACK

With 3¼mm (No 9/US 4) needles cast on 78 sts.

1st rib row (right side) K2, [p2, k2] to end.

2nd rib row P2, [k2, p2] to end.

Rep last 2 rows 3 times more.

Change to 4½mm (No 7/US 7) needles.

Beg with a k row, work in st st until Back measures 13cm/5in from beg, ending with a p row.

Change to 3¾mm (No 9/US 4) needles.

Work 8 rows in rib as given for welt.

Change to 4½mm (No 7/US 7) needles.

Beg with a k row, work in st st until Back measures 43cm/17in from beg, ending with a p row.

Shape Shoulders

Cast off 13 sts at beg of next 4 rows. Cast off rem 26 sts.

LEFT FRONT

With 3¾mm (No 9/US 4) needles cast on 39 sts.

1st rib row (right side) [K2, p2] to last 3 sts, k3.

2nd rib row P3, [k2, p2] to end.

Rep last 2 rows 3 times more.

Change to 4½mm (No 7/US 7) needles.

Beg with a k row, work in st st until Front measures 13cm/5in from beg, ending with a p row.

Change to 3¾mm (No 9/US 4) needles.

Work 8 rows in rib as given for welt.

Change to 4½mm (No 7/US 7) needles.

Beg with a k row, work in st st until Front measures 38cm/15in from beg, ending at front edge.

Shape Neck

Cast off 8 sts at beg of next row. Dec one st at neck edge on next 3 rows and 2 foll alt rows. 26 sts. Cont straight until Front matches Back to shoulder shaping, ending at side edge.

Shape Shoulder

Cast off 13 sts at beg of next row. Work 1 row. Cast off rem 13 sts.

RIGHT FRONT

With 3¾mm (No 9/US 4) needles cast on 39 sts.

1st rib row (right side) K3, [p2, k2] to end.

2nd rib row [P2, k2] to last 3 sts, p3. Complete as given for Left Front.

SLEEVES

With 3¾mm (No 9/US 4) needles cast on 34 sts.

Work 12 rows in rib as given for Back welt, inc 6 sts evenly across last row. 40 sts.

Change to 4½mm (No 7/US 7) needles.

Beg with a k row, work in st st, inc one st at each end of every 3rd row until there are 68 sts. Cont straight until work measures 24cm/9½in from beg, ending with a p row. Cast off.

PATCH POCKETS (make 4)

With 4½mm (No 7/US 7) needles cast on 22 sts.

Beg with a k row, work 20 rows in st st. Change to 3¾mm (No 9/US 4) needles.

Work 2 rows in rib as given for Back welt.

Buttonhole row Rib 10, cast off 2, rib to end.

Next row Rib to end, casting on 2 sts over the cast off sts in previous row. Rib 2 rows more. Cast off in rib.

BUTTONHOLE BAND

With 3¾mm (No 9/US 4) needles and right side facing, k up 74 sts along front edge of Right Front. Work 3 rows in rib as given for Back welt.

Buttonhole row Rib 4, [cast off 2, rib 10 sts more] 5 times, cast off 2, rib to end.

Next row Rib to end, casting on 2 sts over those cast off in previous row. Rib 2 rows more. Cast off in rib.

BUTTON BAND

With 3¾mm (No 9/US 4) needles and right side facing, k up 74 sts along front edge of Left Front. Work 7 rows in rib as given for Back welt. Cast off in rib.

COLLAR

Join shoulder seams.

With 3¾mm (No 9/US 4) needles, right side facing and beginning in line with buttonholes, k up 25 sts up right front neck, 26 sts across back neck and 25 sts down left front neck to centre of button band. 76 sts.

1st rib row K3, [p1, k2] to last 4 sts, p1, k3.

2nd rib row K1, [p2, k1] to end.

Next 2 rows Rib to last 21 sts, turn.

Next 2 rows Rib to last 17 sts, turn.

Next 2 rows Rib to last 13 sts, turn.

Next 2 rows Rib to last 9 sts, turn. Rib to end.

Inc row K1, [p2, k twice in next st] to last 3 sts, p2, k1. 100 sts.

Next row K3, [p2, k2] to last 5 sts, p2, k3.

Rib 11 rows more. Cast off loosely in rib.

TO MAKE UP

Sew one patch pocket on each front and each sleeve. Sew on sleeves, placing centre of sleeves to shoulder seams. Join side and sleeve seams. Sew on buttons.

ROLLED-EDGE JACKET

MATERIALS

3(3:4:4) 100g hanks of Rowan Magpie.
Pair of 4½mm (No 7/US 7) knitting
needles.
4 buttons.

TENSION

18 sts and 26 rows to 10cm/4in square
over st st on 4½mm (No 7/US 7)
needles.

ABBREVIATIONS

See page 8.

BACK

With 4½mm (No 7/US 7) needles cast
on 50(56:64:70) sts.
Beg with a k row, work in st st until
Back measures 27(32:37:42)cm/10¾
(12½:14½:16½)in from beg, ending with
a p row.

Shape Shoulders

Cast off 14(16:19:22) sts at beg of next
2 rows. Cast off rem 22(24:26:26) sts.

POCKET LININGS (MAKE 2)

With 4½mm (No 7/US 7) needles cast
on 15(17:19:21) sts.
Beg with a k row, work 19(21:23:25)
rows in st st. Leave these sts on a
holder.

LEFT FRONT

With 4½mm (No 7/US 7) needles cast
on 27(30:34:37) sts.
1st row (right side) K.
2nd row K4, p to end.
These 2 rows form st st with 4 sts at
front edge in garter st. Work a further
24(26:28:30) rows as set.

Place pocket

Next row K5(5:6:6), cast off next
15(17:19:21) sts, k to end.
Next row K4, p3(4:5:6), p across sts of
pocket lining, p to end.
Cont straight until work measures
15(19:22:25)cm/6(7½:8½:10)in from

beg, ending with a wrong-side row.

Shape Collar

Next row K to last 4 sts, m1, k4.
Working inc st into st st, work 3 rows
straight. Rep last 4 rows 5(6:6:7) times
more. 33(37:41:45) sts. Cont straight
until Front matches Back to shoulder
shaping, ending at side edge.

Shape Shoulder

Next row Cast off 14(16:19:22) sts, k
to end.
Work on rem 19(21:22:23) sts for back
collar as follows:
Next row K4, p to end.
Next row K.
Next 2 rows K4, p6(7:8:9), turn and k

MEASUREMENTS

To fit age	6	12	24	36 months	
Actual chest measurement	56	62	71	78	cm
	22	24½	28	30¾	in
Length	27	32	37	42	cm
	10¾	12½	14½	16½	in
Sleeve seam	18	21	24	28	cm
	7	8¼	9½	11	in

to end.

Rep last 4 rows 3(4:5:5) times more.
Work 1 row across all sts. Cast off.
Mark front edge to indicate buttons:
first one to come 4 rows up from
lower edge, last one 4 rows below
collar shaping and rem 2 evenly spaced
between.

RIGHT FRONT

With 4½mm (No 7/US 7) needles cast
on 27(30:34:37) sts.
1st row (right side) K.
2nd row P to last 4 sts, k4.
These 2 rows form st st with 4 sts at
front edge in garter st.
Work 2 more rows as set.
Buttonhole row (right side) K1,
k2tog, yf, k to end.
Work 21(23:25:27) rows, making
buttonhole to match marker on Left
Front as before.
Place Pocket

Next row K7(8:9:10), cast off next
15(17:19:21) sts, k to end.
Next row P5(5:6:6), p across sts of
pocket lining, p3(4:5:6), k4.
Cont straight until Right Front matches
Left Front to beg of collar shaping,
ending with a wrong side row, making
buttonholes at markers as before.
Shape Collar
Next row K4, m1, k to end.
Working inc st into st st, work 3 rows
straight. Rep last 4 rows 5(6:6:7) times
more. 33(37:41:45) sts. Cont straight
until Front matches Back to shoulder
shaping, ending at side edge.
Shape Shoulder
Next row Cast off 14(16:19:22), p to
last 4 sts, k4.
Work on rem 19(21:22:23) sts for
collar as follows:
Next row K.
Next row P to last 4 sts, k4.
Next 2 rows K10(11:12:13), turn, p to

last 4 sts, k4.
Rep last 4 rows 3(4:5:5) times more.
Work 1 row across all sts. Cast off.

SLEEVES

With 4½mm (No 7/US 7) needles cast
on 30(30:32:32) sts.
Beg with a k row, work in st st, inc one
st at each end of 7th row, 4(5:0:0) foll
3rd rows, then on every foll 4th row
until there are 50(54:58:62) sts. Cont
straight until sleeve measures
18(21:24:28)cm/7(8¼:9½:11)in from
beg, ending with a p row. Cast off.

TO MAKE UP

Catch down pocket linings. Join
shoulder seams and back seam of
collar. Sew back collar to back neck
edge. Sew on sleeves, placing centre of
sleeves to shoulder seams. Join side
and sleeve seams. Sew on buttons.

SHAWL-COLLARED FAIR ISLE CARDIGAN

MATERIALS

3(4:5) 50g balls of Rowan Cotton
Glace in Navy (A).
1 ball of same in each Blue, Cream,
Yellow and Rust.
Pair each of 3mm (No 11/US 2) and
3¼mm (No 10/US 3) knitting needles.
4 buttons.

TENSION

26 sts and 33 rows to 10cm/4in square
over pattern on 3¼mm (No 10/US 3)
needles.

ABBREVIATIONS

See page 8.

NOTES

Read chart from right to left on right
side rows and from left to right on

MEASUREMENTS

To fit age	6	12	24 months	
Actual chest measurement	58	65	73	cm
	22¾	25½	28¾	in
Length	29	33	37	cm
	11½	13	14½	in
Sleeve seam	18	20	22	cm
	7	8	8¾	in

wrong side rows. When working in
pattern, strand yarn not in use loosely
across wrong side of work to keep
fabric elastic.

BACK AND FRONTS

Worked in one piece to armholes.
With 3mm (No 11/US 2) needles and
A, cast on 155(175:195) sts.
Next row K1, [p1, k1] to end.
This row forms moss st. Moss st 1 row.

Buttonhole row (right side) Patt 2,
yrn, p2tog, patt to end.
Moss st 3 rows.
Change to 3¼mm (No 10/US 3)
needles.
Using separate small balls of A at each
end and twisting yarns together on
wrong side when changing colours,
work in patt from chart as follows:
1st row (right side) With A, moss st
5, k across 10 st rep of 1st row of

chart to last 10 sts, k 5 edge sts of chart, with A, moss st 5.

2nd row With A, moss st 5, p across 5 edge sts of 2nd row of chart, then p across 10 st rep to last 5 sts, with A, moss st 5.

Cont in patt from chart as set until work measures 17(19:21)cm/6¾(7½: 8¼)in from beg, ending with a wrong side row, **at the same time**, make 3 more buttonholes as before 5(5.5:6)cm/2(2¼:2½)in from previous buttonhole.

Right Front

Next row Moss st 5 and leave these 5 sts on a safety pin, patt 35(40:45), turn. Work on this set of sts only.

Shape Neck

Keeping patt correct, dec one st at neck edge on every 3rd row until 24(28:32) sts rem. Cont straight until Front measures 29(33:37)cm/11½(13: 14½)in from beg, ending at armhole edge.

Shape Shoulder

Cast off 12(14:16) sts at beg of next row. Work 1 row. Cast off rem 12(14:16) sts.

Back

With right side facing, rejoin yarn to rem sts, patt 75(85:95) sts, turn. Work straight on this set of sts only until Back matches Front to shoulder shaping, ending with a wrong side row.

Shape Shoulders

Cast off 12(14:16) sts at beg of next 4 rows. Leave rem 27(29:31) sts on a holder.

Left Front

With right side facing, rejoin yarn to rem sts and patt to last 5 sts, turn: leave the 5 sts on a safety pin.
Complete as given for Right Front.

SLEEVES

With 3mm (No 11/US 2) needles and A, cast on 35(37:41) sts.
Work 5 rows in moss st as given for Back and Fronts.
Next row Moss st 4(4:1), m1, [moss

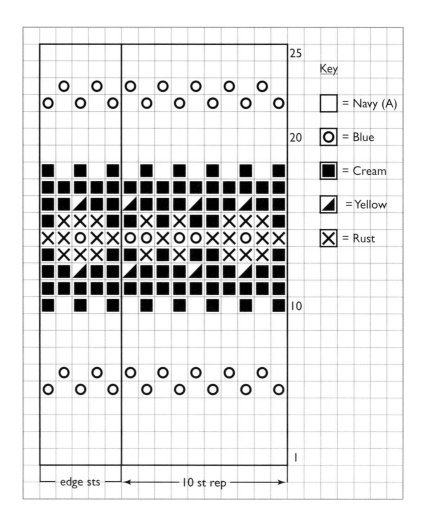

Key

☐	= Navy (A)
Ⓞ	= Blue
■	= Cream
◢	= Yellow
☒	= Rust

edge sts ←— 10 st rep —→

st 3(4:3), m1] to last 4(5:1) sts, moss st to end. 45(45:55) sts.
Change to 3¼mm (No 10/US 3) needles.
Beg with a k row, work in st st and patt from chart, **at the same time**, inc one st at each end of 3rd row and every foll 4th(3rd:4th) row until there are 65(73:81) sts, working inc sts into patt. Cont straight until Sleeve measures 18(20:22)cm/7(8:8¾)in from beg, ending with a wrong-side row. Cast off.

LEFT COLLAR

Join shoulder seams.
With 3mm (No 11/US 2) needles, rejoin A yarn at inside edge to 5 sts on left front safety pin, inc in first st, moss

st to end. Cont in moss st, inc one st at inside edge on every foll 4th row until there are 21 sts. Cont straight until shaped edge of collar fits left front neck to shoulder, ending at outside edge.
Next 2 rows Moss st 12, turn, sl 1, moss st to end.
Moss st 6 rows. Rep last 8 rows until collar fits left front neck to centre of back neck. Cast off.

RIGHT COLLAR

Work as given for Left Collar.

TO MAKE UP

Join back seam of collar and sew collar in place. Sew in sleeves, placing centre of sleeves to shoulder seams. Join sleeve seams. Sew on buttons.

DOUBLE-BREASTED JACKET

MATERIALS
6(7) 100g balls of Rowan Super Chunky Tweed.
Pair each of 7½mm (No 1/US 10½) and 8mm (No 0/US 11) knitting needles.
4 buttons.

MEASUREMENTS

To fit age	2-3	4-5	years
Actual chest	81	91	cm
measurement	32	36	in
Length	41	46	cm
	16	18	in
Sleeve seam	25	30	cm
	10	12	in

TENSION
12 sts and 19 rows to 10cm/4in square over moss st on 8mm (No 0/US 11) needles.

ABBREVIATIONS
See page 8.

BACK
With 7½mm (No 1/US 10½) needles cast on 49(55) sts.
1st rib row (right side) K1, [p1, k1] to end.
2nd rib row P1, [k1, p1] to end.
Rep last 2 rows twice more.
Change to 8mm (No 0/US 11) needles.
1st row P1, [k1, p1] to end.
This row forms moss st patt. Cont in moss st until work measures 41(46)cm/16(18)in from beg, ending with a wrong side row.

Shape Shoulders
Cast off 8(9) sts at beg of next 2 rows and 9(10) sts at beg of foll 2 rows.
Leave rem 15(17) sts on a holder.

LEFT FRONT
With 7½mm (No 1/US 10½) needles cast on 17(19) sts.
Work 6 rows in rib as given for Back.
Change to 8mm (No 0/US 11) needles.
Work in moss st as given for Back until front measures same as Back to shoulder shaping, ending with a wrong side row.

Shape Shoulder
Cast off 8(9) sts at beg of next row.
Work 1 row. Cast off rem 9(10) sts.

RIGHT FRONT
Work as given for Left Front, reversing shoulder shaping.

SLEEVES
With 7½mm (No 1/US 10½) needles cast on 18(20) sts.
Work 6 rows in k1, p1 rib.
Inc row Rib 3(1), m1, [rib 2(3), m1] 6 times rib 3(1). 25(27) sts.
Change to 8mm (No 0/US 11) needles.
Work in moss st as given for Back, inc one st at each end of 3rd row and every foll 5th row until there are 39(43) sts, working inc sts into moss st.
Cont straight until sleeve measures 25(30)cm/10(12)in from beg, ending with a wrong side row. Cast off.

FRONT BANDS AND COLLAR
Join shoulder seams.
With 7½mm (No 1/US 10½) needles and right side facing, k up 51(61) sts along front edge of Right Front to shoulder, work across back neck as follows: k2(1), m1, [k2(3), m1] 5 times, k3(1), k up 51(61) sts down front edge of Left Front to cast on edge. 123(145) sts.
1st rib row K1, [p1, k1] to end.
2nd rib row P1, [k1, p1] to end.
Next row Rib 76(88), turn.
Next row Rib 29(31), turn.
Next row Rib 33(35), turn.
Next row Rib 37(39) turn.
Cont in this way, working 4 sts more at end of every row on the next 6(8) rows, turn and rib to end. Rib 2 rows across all sts.
Buttonholes row Rib 2, yf, k2tog, rib 16(20), yf, k2tog, rib to end.
Rib 11(13) rows. Rep the buttonholes row again. Rib 3 rows. Cast off in rib.

TO MAKE UP
Sew in sleeves, placing centre of sleeves to shoulder seams. Join side and sleeve seams. Sew on buttons.

Shawl-collared Sweater

MATERIALS

4(5) 100g balls of Rowan Super Chunky Tweed.
Pair each of 8mm (No 0/US 11) and 9mm (No 00/US 12) knitting needles.

MEASUREMENTS

To fit age	2-3	4-5 years	
Actual chest	84	92	cm
measurement	33	36¼	in
Length	43	48	cm
	17	19	in
Sleeve seam	28	32	cm
	11	12½	in

TENSION

10 sts and 15 rows to 10cm/4in square over st st on 9mm (No 00/US 12) needles.

ABBREVIATIONS

See page 8.

BACK

With 8mm (No 0/US 11) needles cast on 42(46) sts.
Work 4 rows in k1, p1 rib.
Change to 9mm (No 00/US 12) needles.
Beg with a k row, work in st st until Back measures 43(48)cm/17(19)in from beg, ending with a p row.

Shape Shoulders

Cast off 15(16) sts at beg of next 2 rows. Cast off rem 12(14) sts.

FRONT

Work as given for Back until Front measures 27(31)cm/10¾(12¼)in from beg, ending with a p row.

Shape Neck

Next row K21(23), turn.
Work on this set of sts only.
Next row P.
Next row K to last 4 sts, k2tog, k2.
Next row P.
Next row K.
Next row P2, p2tog, p to end.
Next row K.
Rep last 6 rows twice more, then work first 1(3) rows of the 6 rows again. 15(16) sts.
Cont straight until Front measures 43(48)cm/17(19)in from beg, ending at side edge. Cast off.
With right side facing, join yarn to rem sts and k to end.
Next row P.
Next row K2, skpo, k to end.
Next row P.
Next row K.
Next row P to last 4 sts, p2tog tbl, p2.
Next row K.
Complete as given for first side of neck.

SLEEVES

With 8mm (No 0/US 11) needles cast on 18(20) sts.
Work 6 rows in k1, p1 rib, inc 2 sts evenly across last row. 20(22) sts.
Change to 9mm (No 00/US 12) needles.
Beg with a k row, work 2 rows in st st.
Next row K1, k twice in next st, k to last 3 sts, k twice in next st, k2.
Work 3 rows in st st. Rep last 4 rows 7(8) times more. 36(40) sts. Cont straight for a few rows until work measures 28(32)cm/11(12½)in from beg, ending with a p row. Cast off.

COLLAR

With 8mm (No 0/US 11) needles cast on 16(18) sts.
Work 1 row in k1, p1 rib. Cont in k1, p1 rib, casting on 4 sts at beg of next 10 rows. 56(58) sts. Rib 4 rows. Cast off loosely.

TO MAKE UP

Join shoulder seams. Beginning at centre of front neck, sew cast on edge of collar to neck edge. Lap right side of collar over left at centre front and sew row ends edges of collar to neck edge. Sew on sleeves, placing centre of sleeves to shoulder seams. Join side and sleeve seams.

Moss stitch tunic

MATERIALS

4(4:5) 100g hanks of Rowan Magpie. Pair each of 4½mm (No 7/US 7) and 5mm (No 6/US 8) knitting needles.

TENSION

18 sts and 32 rows to 10cm/4in square over moss st on 5mm (No 6/US 8) needles.

ABBREVIATIONS

See page 8.

BACK

With 5mm (No 6/US 8) needles cast on 55(63:71) sts.
1st row K1, [p1, k1] to end.
This row forms moss st. Cont in moss st until back measures 32(36:41)cm/12½ (14:16)in from beg.
Shape Shoulders
Cast off 8(10:11) sts at beg of next 2 rows and 9(10:12) sts at beg of foll 2 rows. Leave rem 21(23:25) sts on a holder.

FRONT

Work as given for Back until Front measures 27(30:35)cm/10½(11¾:13¾)in from beg.
Shape Neck
Next row Moss st 22(25:29), turn.
Work on this set of sts only. Dec one st at neck edge on next 2 rows, then on every foll alt row until 17(20:23) sts

rem. Cont straight until Front matches Back to shoulder shaping, ending at side edge.
Shape Shoulder
Cast off 8(10:11) sts at beg of next row. Work 1 row. Cast off rem 9(10:12) sts.
With right side facing, slip centre 11(13:13) sts onto a holder, rejoin yarn to rem sts and moss st to end.
Complete to match first side.

SLEEVES

With 5mm (No 6/US 8) needles cast on 27(29:31) sts.
Work 14(16:16) rows in moss st as given for Back for cuff.
Change to 4½mm (No 7/US 7) needles.
Moss st 14(16:16) rows.
Change to 5mm (No 6/US 8) needles.
Cont in moss st, inc one st at each end of every 3rd row until there are 51(55:61) sts. Cont straight until sleeve

measures 24(27:29)cm/9½(10¾:11½)in from beg. Cast off.

NECKBAND

Join right shoulder seam.
With 4½mm (No 7/US 7) needles and right side facing, k up 14(15:15) sts down left front neck, moss st centre front sts, k up 14(14:15) sts up right front neck, moss st back neck sts. 60(65:68) sts. Work 13(17:17) rows in moss st.
Change to 5mm (No 6/US 8) needles. Moss st 14(18:18) rows. Cast off in moss st.

TO MAKE UP

Join right shoulder and neckband seam, reversing seam half way up on neckband. Sew on sleeves, placing centre of sleeves to shoulder seams. Beginning 4cm/1½in up from lower edge, join side then sleeve seams, reversing seam on cuffs. Turn back cuffs.

MEASUREMENTS				
To fit age	**1**	**2**	**3 years**	
Actual chest measurement	61	70	79	cm
	24	27½	31	in
Length	32	36	41	cm
	12½	14	16	in
Sleeve seam	20	22	24	cm
(with cuff turned back)	8	8¾	9½	in

STOCKING STITCH SWEATER

MATERIALS

6(6:7:8) 50g balls of Rowan DK Handknit Cotton.
Pair each of 3¼mm (No 10/US 3) and 4mm (No 8/US 6) knitting needles.
2 buttons and medium size crochet hook (optional).

TENSION

20 sts and 28 rows to 10cm/4in square over st st on 4mm (No 8/US 6) needles.

ABBREVIATIONS

See page 8.

BACK

With 4mm (No 8/US 6) needles cast on 56(62:70:78) sts.
Beg with a k row, work in st st until back measures 25(30:35:40)cm/10(11¾: 13¾:15¾)in from beg, ending with a p row.

Shape Shoulders

Cast off 8(9:11:12) sts at beg of next 2 rows and 8(9:10:12) sts at beg of foll 2 rows. Leave rem 24(26:28:30) sts on a holder.

FRONT

Work as given for Back until Front measures 20(25:30:35)cm/8(9¾:11¾: 13¾)in from beg, ending with a p row.

Shape Neck

Next row K23(25:28:31), turn. Work on this set of sts only. Dec one st at neck edge on next 7 rows. 16(18:21:24) sts. Cont straight until Front matches Back to shoulder shaping, ending at side edge.

Shape Shoulder

Cast off 8(9:11:12) sts at beg of next row. Work 1 row. Cast off rem 8(9:10:12) sts.
With right side facing, slip centre 10(12:14:16) sts onto a holder, rejoin yarn to rem sts and k to end. Complete to match first side.

SLEEVES

With 4mm (No 8/US 6) needles cast on 34(38:42:46) sts.
Beg with a k row, work in st st, inc one st at each end of 5th row and every foll 4th(5th:6th:6th) row until there are 52(56:60:64) sts. Cont straight until sleeve measures 16(19:22:25)cm/6¼ (7½:8¾:10)in from beg, ending with a p row. Cast off.

NECKBAND

Join right shoulder seam.
With 3¼mm (No 10/US 3) needles and right side facing, k up 15 sts down left front neck, k centre front sts, k up 15 sts up right front neck, k back neck sts. 64(68:72:76) sts. Beg with a p row, work 7 rows in st st. Cast off knitwise.

TO MAKE UP

Join left shoulder and neckband seam, reversing seam on neckband or on smaller sizes join left shoulder to within 5 sts of neckband. With crochet hook, make 2 buttonhole loops along front edge of shoulder and neckband opening. Sew on buttons. Sew on sleeves, placing centre of sleeves to shoulder seams. Join side and sleeve seams.

MEASUREMENTS

To fit age	6	12	24	36 months	
Actual chest measurement	56	62	70	78	cm
	22	24½	27½	30¾	in
Length	25	30	35	40	cm
	10	11¾	13¾	15¾	in
Sleeve seam	16	19	22	25	cm
	6¼	7½	8¾	10	in

TRIANGLE-EDGED CARDIGAN AND BOOTEES

MATERIALS
For the set 4(5:6) 50g balls of Jaeger Pure Cotton.
Pair each of 2¾mm (No 12/US 2), 3mm (No 11/US 2) and 3¼mm (No 10/US 3) knitting needles.
3 buttons for Cardigan, 2 buttons for Bootees.

TENSION
25 sts and 34 rows to 10cm/4in square over st st on 3¼mm (No 10/US 3) needles.

ABBREVIATIONS
See page 8.

CARDIGAN
BACK AND FRONTS
Knitted in one piece to armholes.
With 3¼mm (No 10/US 3) needles cast on 153(161:169) sts.
K 5 rows.
Work border pattern as follows:
1st row and 3 foll alt rows (right side) K.
2nd row K4, p1, [k7, p1] to last 4 sts, k4.
4th row K4, p2, [k5, p3] to last 11 sts, k5, p2, k4.
6th row K4, p3, [k3, p5] to last 10 sts, k3, p3, k4.
8th row K4, p4, [k1, p7] to last 9 sts, k1, p4, k4.
9th row K.
10th row K4, p to last 4 sts, k4.
Keeping the 4 sts at front edges in garter st (every row k) and remainder in st st, cont until work measures 13(14:15)cm/5¼(5½:5¾)in from beg, ending with a right side row.
Left Front
Next row K4, p35(37:39), turn.
Work on this set of sts only until Front measures 20(22:23)cm/8(8¾:9)in from beg, ending at front edge.

Shape Neck
Next row Work across first 9 sts and leave these 9 sts on a safety pin, work to end.
Dec one st at neck edge on every row until 22(23:24) sts rem. Cont straight until work measures 24(26:28)cm/9½ (10¼:11)in from beg, ending at armhole edge.
Shape Shoulder
Cast off 11(11:12) sts at beg of next row. Work 1 row. Cast off rem 11(12:12) sts.
Back
With wrong side facing, rejoin yarn to rem sts, p75(79:83), turn. Work on this set of sts only until Back measures same as Left Front to shoulder shaping, ending with a p row.
Shape Shoulders
Cast off 11(11:12) sts at beg of next 2 rows and 11(12:12) sts at beg of foll 2 rows. Leave rem 31(33:35) sts on a holder.
Mark front edge of Left Front to indicate position of 3 buttons: first one 13(14:15)cm/5¼(5½:5¾)in from beg, last one 1cm/¼in below neck shaping and remaining one place half way between.
Right Front
With wrong side facing, rejoin yarn to rem sts and p to last 4 sts, k4.
Buttonhole row (right side) K1,

k2tog, yf, k to end.
Complete as given for Left Front, making buttonholes at markers as before.

SLEEVES
With 3mm (No 11/US 2) needles cast on 33(37:41) sts.
K 5 rows.
Change to 3¼mm (No 10/US 3) needles.
Work border patt as follows:
1st row and 3 foll alt rows (right side) K.
2nd row K4(6:4), p1, [k7, p1] to last 4(6:4) sts, k4(6:4).
4th row K3(5:3), p3, [k5, p3] to last 3(5:3) sts, k3(5:3).
6th row K2(4:2), p5, [k3, p5] to last 2(4:2) sts, k2(4:2).
8th row P0(2:0), [k1, p7] to last 1(3:1) sts, k1, p0(2:0).
Beg with a k row, work in st st, inc one st at each end of 1st row and every foll 3rd row until there are 55(61:67) sts.
Work a few rows straight until Sleeve measures 14(16:18)cm/5½(6¼:7)in from beg, ending with a p row. Cast off.

COLLAR
Join shoulder seams.
With 3mm (No 11/US 2) needles and right side facing, slip 9 sts from right

front safety pin onto needle, join in yarn and k up 13(13:15) sts up right front neck, k back neck sts, k up 13(13:15) sts down left front neck, then k9 sts from left front safety pin. 75(77:83) sts. K 1 row.

Next 2 rows Cast off 3, k to end. 69(71:77) sts.

Next row [K3(2:1), m1] 4(1:1) times, [k2, m1, k2(3:3), m1] 11(13:15) times, k1, [m1, k3] 4(1:0) times. 99(99:108) sts.

K 10 rows.

**Next row K9, turn.

Work in garter st on these 9 sts only. Dec one st at each end of next row and 2 foll alt rows. K 1 row.

Next row Sl 1, k2tog, psso and fasten off.

Rejoin yarn to rem sts at base of triangle just made and rep from ** until all sts are worked off.

TO MAKE UP

Sew in sleeves, placing centre of sleeves to shoulder seams. Join sleeve seams. Sew on buttons.

BOOTEES
LEFT BOOTEE

With 3¼mm (No 10/US 3) needles cast on 40 sts.

K 1 row.

Inc row P twice in first st, p18, p twice in each of next 2 sts, p18, p twice in last st.

K 1 row.

Inc row P twice in first st, p20, p twice in each of next 2 sts, p20, p twice in last st.

K 1 row.

Inc row P twice in first st, p22, p twice in each of next 2 sts, p22, p twice in last st. 52 sts.

Work 6 rows in st st.

Shape Instep

Next row K30, skpo, turn.

Next row P9, p2tog, turn.

Next row K9, skpo, turn.

Rep last 2 rows 4 times more, then the first of the 2 rows again.

Next row K to end. 40 sts.

Work 2 rows across all sts.

Shape Back Heel

Next row P8, turn.

Work 7 rows on these 8 sts. Leave these sts on a safety pin.

With wrong side facing, sl next 24 sts onto a holder, rejoin yarn to rem 8 sts and p to end. Work 7 rows on these 8 sts.

Next row P to end, then p across 8 sts of other side of back heel. 16 sts.***

Next row Cast on 22 sts, p to end.

Buttonhole row K to last 3 sts, k2tog, yf, k1.

P 1 row. Cast off knitwise.

****With 2¾mm (No 12/US 2) needles and right side facing, k up 8 sts down inside edge of back heel, k across 24 sts on a holder, k up 8 sts up inside edge of other side of back heel. 40 sts. Cast off knitwise.

With 2¾mm (No 12/US 2) needles, cast on 45 sts for edging. K 4 rows.

**Next row K9, turn.

Work in garter st (every row k) on these 9 sts only. Dec one st at each end of next row and 2 foll alt rows. K 1 row.

Next row Sl 1, k2tog, psso and fasten off.

Rejoin yarn to rem sts at base of triangle just made and rep from ** until all sts are worked off.

Join back heel and sole seam. Sew on cast-on edge of edging to cast-off edge of ankle strap. Sew on button.

RIGHT BOOTEE

Work as given for Left Bootee to ***. P 1 row.

Next row Cast on 22 sts, k to end.

Buttonhole row P to last 3 sts, p2tog, yrn, p1.

K 1 row. Cast off purlwise.

Complete as given for Left Bootee from **** to end.

SWEATER AND BOOTEES WITH PICOT EDGE

MATERIALS

Sweater 4(5:6) 50g balls of Rowan Cotton Glace.
Pair each of 2¾mm (No 12/US 2) and 3¼mm (No 10/US 3) knitting needles.
2 buttons.
Bootees One 50g ball of Rowan Cotton Glace.
Pair each of 2¾mm (No 12/US 2) and 3¼mm (No 10/US 3) knitting needles.

TENSION

25 sts and 34 rows to 10cm/4in square over st st on 3¼mm (No 10/US 3) needles.

ABBREVIATIONS

See page 8.

SWEATER

BACK

With 2¾mm (No 12/US 2) needles cast on 66(72:80) sts.
Work 8(10:12) rows in k1, p1 rib.
Change to 3¼mm (No 10/US 3) needles.
Beg with a k row, work in st st until back measures 25(30:35)cm/10(12: 13¾)in from beg, ending with a p row.
Shape Shoulders
Cast off 9(10:11) sts at beg of next 4 rows. Leave rem 30(32:36) sts on a holder.

FRONT

Work as given for Back until Front measures 17(20:23)cm/6¾(8:9)in from beg, ending with a p row.
Divide for Opening
Next row K30(33:37), turn.
Work on this set of sts only for a further 4(5:6)cm/1¾(2:2½)in, ending at side edge.
Shape Neck
Next row Work to last 5(6:7) sts and leave these 5(6:7) sts on a safety pin. Dec one st at neck edge on every row

until 18(20:22) sts rem. Cont straight until Front matches Back to shoulder shaping, ending at side edge.
Shape Shoulder
Cast off 9(10:11) sts at beg of next row. Work 1 row. Cast off rem 9(10:11) sts.
With right side facing, rejoin yarn to rem sts, cast off centre 6 sts, k to end.
Complete as given for first side.

SLEEVES

With 2¾mm (No 12/US 2) needles cast on 36(40:44) sts.
Work 8(10:12) rows in k1, p1 rib.
Change to 3¼mm (No 10/US 3) needles.
Beg with a k row, work in st st, inc one st at each end of every 3rd row until there are 58(66:74) sts. Cont straight until work measures 15(18:22)cm/6(7: 8¾)in from beg, ending with a p row. Cast off.

BUTTON BAND

With 2¾mm (No 12/US 2) needles and right side facing, k up 15(17:19) sts along left edge of front opening.
1st rib row K1, [p1, k1] to end.
2nd rib row P1, [k1, p1] to end.
Rib 5 rows more. Cast off in rib.

BUTTONHOLE BAND

With 2¾mm (No 12/US 2) needles and

right side facing, k up 15(17:19) sts along right edge of front opening.
1st rib row K1, [p1, k1] to end.
2nd rib row P1, [k1, p1] to end.
Rib 1 row more.
Buttonhole row Rib2, yf, k2tog, rib 7(9:11), yrn, p2tog, rib2.
Rib 3 rows, dec 2 sts evenly across last row. 13(15:17) sts.
Cast off row Cast off knitwise 1 st, *slip st used in casting off back onto left hand needle, cast on 2 sts, cast off 4 sts knitwise; rep from * until all sts are worked off. Fasten off.

COLLAR

Join shoulder seams.
With 2¾mm (No 12/US 2) needles, right side facing, and beg in line with buttonholes, k up 3 sts from buttonhole band, k sts from right front safety pin, k up 16(18:20) sts up right front neck, k back neck sts inc one st at centre, k up 16(18:20) sts down left front neck, k sts from left front safety pin, then k up 3 sts to centre of button band. 79(87:97) sts.
Work in rib as given for Button Band for 1 row.
Next 2 rows Rib to last 20(24:28) sts, turn.
Next 2 rows Rib to last 16(20:24) sts, turn.
Next 2 rows Rib to last 12(16:20) sts, turn.

MEASUREMENTS

Sweater

To fit age	3-6	6-12	12-18 months	
Actual chest measurement	53	58	64	cm
	21	23	25	in
Length	25	30	35	cm
	10	12	13¾	in
Sleeve seam	15	18	22	cm
	6	7	8¾	in

Bootees

To fit age	0-9 months

Cont in this way, working 4 sts more at end of every row, work 2(4:6) rows.

Next row Rib to end.

Rib 10(12:14) rows. Break off yarn.

Next row With right side of collar facing, k up 7(8:9) sts along row ends edge of collar, rib the sts on needle, then k up 7(8:9) sts along row ends edge of collar. Work cast off row as given for Buttonhole Band.

TO MAKE UP

Sew on sleeves, placing centre of sleeves to shoulder seams. Join side and sleeve seams. Lap Buttonhole Band over Button Band and catch down row ends edges to base of opening. Sew on buttons.

BOOTEES
TO MAKE

With 2¾mm (No 12/US 2) needles cast on 26 sts. K 1 row.

1st row K1, yf, k11, [yf, k1] twice, yf, k11, yf, k1.

2nd row and 3 foll alt rows K to end, working tbl into yf of previous row.

3rd row K2, yf, k11, yf, k2, yf, k3, yf, k11, yf, k2.

5th row K3, yf, k11, [yf, k4] twice, yf, k11, yf, k3.

7th row K4, yf, k11, yf, k5, yf, k6, yf, k11, yf, k4.

9th row K5, yf, k11, [yf, k7] twice, yf, k11, yf, k5. 51 sts.

10th row As 2nd row.

Change to 3¼mm (No 10/US 3) needles.

Beg with a k row, work 7 rows in st st.

Change to 2¾mm (No 12/US 2) needles.

K 3 rows.

Change to 3¼mm (No 10/US 3) needles.

Shape Instep

Next row K29, skpo, turn.

Next row Sl 1, p7, p2tog, turn.

Next row Sl 1, k7, skpo, turn.

Rep last 2 rows 5 times more, then work 1st of these 2 rows again.

Next row Sl 1, k7, skpo, k to end.

Next row P21, p2tog, p to end.

35 sts. K1 row. P 1 row.

Next row K1, [p1, k1] to end.

Next row P1, [k1, p1] to end.

Rep last 2 rows 3 times more, then work 1st of these 2 rows again.

Next row Rib 17, cast off 1 st, rib to end.

Rib 11 rows on last set of 17 sts for one side of cuff. Break off yarn.

With 2¾mm (No 12/US 2) needles and right side of cuff facing, k up 8 sts along row ends edge of cuff, then rib sts on needle.

Cast off row Cast off knitwise 1 st, *slip st used in casting off back onto left hand needle, cast on 2 sts, cast off 4 sts knitwise; rep from * until all sts are worked off. Fasten off.

Rejoin yarn at centre to rem 17 sts and rib 11 rows.

Change to 2¾mm (No 12 /US 2) needles.

Next row Rib to end, then k up 8 sts along row ends edge of cuff.

Work cast off row.

Join sole and back seam, reversing seam on cuff.

Turn back cuff.

Make one more.

RIBBED SWEATER

MATERIALS

5(6:6) 50g balls of Rowan DK Handknit Cotton in Blue (A).
2(3:3) balls of same in Cream (B).
Pair each of 3¼mm (No 10/US 3) and 4mm (No 8/US 6) knitting needles.

TENSION

20 sts and 32 rows to 10cm/4in square over pattern on 4mm (No 8/US 6) needles.

ABBREVIATIONS

See page 8.

BACK

With 3¼mm (No 10/US 3) needles and A, cast on 63(73:83) sts.
1st row (right side) K3, [p2, k3] to end.
2nd row P.
These 2 rows form patt. Patt 3 rows more.
Change to 4mm (No 8/US 6) needles and B.
Beg with 2nd row, work in patt until Back measures 14(16:18)cm/5½(6¼:7)in from beg, ending with 1st patt row.
Change to A and cont in patt until Back measures 30(34:38)cm/11¾(13½:15)in from beg, ending with 2nd patt row.
Shape Shoulders
Cast off 9(11:13) sts at beg of next 4 rows. Leave rem 27(29:31) sts on a holder.

FRONT

Work as given for Back until Front measures 25(29:33)cm/9¾(11½:13)in from beg, ending with 2nd patt row.
Shape Neck
Next row Patt 26(30:34), turn.

Work on this set of sts only. Dec one st at neck edge on next 8 rows.
18(22:26) sts. Cont straight until Front matches Back to shoulder shaping, ending at side edge.
Shape Shoulder
Cast off 9(11:13) sts at beg of next row. Work 1 row. Cast off rem 9 (11:13) sts.
With right side facing, slip centre 11(13:15) sts onto a holder, rejoin yarn to rem sts and patt to end. Complete to match first side.

SLEEVES

With 3¼mm (No 10/US 3) needles and B, cast on 38(43:43) sts.
1st rib row P3, [k2, p3] to end.
2nd rib row K3, [p2, k3] to end.
Rib 13 rows more for cuff.
Beg with 1st row (thus reversing fabric), rib another 14 rows.
Change to 4mm (No 8/US 6) needles and A.
Beg with 2nd row, work in patt as given for Back, inc one st at each end of 2nd row and every foll 4th row until there are 56(63:67) sts. Cont straight until sleeve measures 24(27:30)cm/9½(10¾: 11¾)in from beg, ending with 2nd patt row. Cast off.

NECKBAND

Join right shoulder seam.
With 3¼mm (No 10/US 3) needles, right side facing and A, k up17(16:18) sts down left front neck, patt across centre front sts, k up 16(14:17) sts up right front neck, patt across back neck sts. 71(72:81) sts.
1st rib row P0(1:2), [k2, p3] to last 1(1:4) sts, k1(1:2), p0(0:2).
2nd rib row K0(0:2), p1(1:2), [k3, p2] to last 0(1:2) sts, k0(1:2).
Rib 8 rows more.
Next row K0(1:2), [p2, k3] to last 1(1:4) sts, p1(1:2), k0(0:2).
Next row P0(0:2), k1(1:2), [p3, k2] to last 0(1:2) sts, p0(1:2).
Rib a further 5 rows as set.
Change to B and p 1 row, then rib another 4 rows. Cast off in rib.

TO MAKE UP

Join right shoulder and neckband seam, reversing seam half way on neckband. Sew on sleeves, placing centre of sleeves to shoulder seams. Join side and sleeve seams, reversing seams on cuffs. Turn back cuffs.

MEASUREMENTS				
To fit age	**1**	**2**	**3 years**	
Actual chest measurement	63	73	83	cm
	24¾	28¾	32½	in
Length	30	34	38	cm
	11¾	13½	15	in
Sleeve seam	19	22	25	cm
(with cuff turned back)	7½	8¾	9¾	in

STRIPED TOP

MATERIALS

3(3:4:4) 50g balls of Rowan Cotton
Glace in Navy (A).
2(2:3:3) balls of same in Cream (B).
Pair each of 2¾mm (No 12/US 2) and
3¼mm (No 10/US 3) knitting needles.
2 buttons.

TENSION

25 sts and 34 rows to 10cm/4in square
over st st on 3¼mm (No 10/US 3)
needles.

ABBREVIATIONS

See page 8.

BACK

With 2¾mm (No 12/US 2) needles
and A, cast on 75(85:95:109) sts.
K 7 rows.
Change to 3¼mm (No 10/US 3)
needles.
1st row (right side) With A, k to
end.
2nd row With A, k3, p to last 3 sts, k3.
3rd and 4th rows As 1st and 2nd
rows.
Using a separate length of A at each
end and twisting yarns together on
wrong side when changing colour, work
as follows:
5th row K3A, with B, k to last 3 sts,
k3A.
6th row K3A, with B, p to last 3 sts,
k3A.
Beg with a k row, work in st st across
all sts and stripe patt of 2 rows A, 2
rows B, 4 rows A, 2 rows B throughout
until back measures 24(28:33:40)cm/9½
(11:13:15¾)in from beg, ending with a
p row.
Shape Neck
Next row K22(26:29:34), turn.
Work on this set of sts only for 9 rows.
Shape Shoulder
Change to 2¾mm (No12/US 2)
needles.

Cont in A only, k 3 rows. Cast off
knitwise.
With 3¼mm (no 10/US 3) needles and
right side facing, slip centre 31
(33:37:41) sts onto a holder, join in yarn
to rem sts and k to end. Work 9 rows.
Shape Shoulder
Change to 2¾mm (No 12/US 2)
needles.
Cont in A only, k 5 rows. Cast off
knitwise.

FRONT

Work as given for Back until Front
measures 22(26:31:38)cm/8¾(10¼:12¼:
15)in from beg, ending with a p row.
Shape Neck
Next row K22(26:29:34), turn.
Work on this set of sts only until Front
matches Back to shoulder shaping,
ending with a p row.
Shape Shoulder
Change to 2¾mm (No 12/US 2)
needles.
Cont in A only, k 2 rows.
Buttonhole row K14(16:18:21),
k2tog, yf, k to end.
K 2 rows. Cast off knitwise.
With 3¼mm (no 10/US 3) needles and
right side facing, sl centre 31(33:37:41)
sts onto a holder, join in yarn to rem
sts and k to end. Cont until Front
matches Back to shoulder shaping,
ending with a p row.
Shape Shoulder
Change to 2¾mm (No 12/US 2)
needles.

Cont in A only, k 3 rows. Cast off
knitwise.

SLEEVES

With 2¾mm (No 12/US 2) needles and
A, cast on 42(46:46:50) sts.
1st rib row (right side) K2, [p2, k2]
to end.
2nd rib row P2, [k2, p2] to end.
Rep last 2 rows 4(4:5:5) times more,
then work 1st row again.
Inc row Rib 3(5:6:2), m1, [rib 4(4:3:5),
m1] 9(9:11:9) times, rib to end.
52(56:58:60) sts.
Change to 3¼mm (No 10/US 3)
needles.
Beg with a k row, work in st st and
stripe patt of 2 rows B, 2 rows A, 2
rows B, 4 rows A throughout, **at the
same time**, inc one st at each end of
every 5th row until there are
62(68:74:78) sts. Cont straight until
sleeve measures
16(18:21:24)cm/6¼(7:8¼:9½)in from
beg, ending with a p row.
Cast off.

NECKBAND

Join right shoulder seam.
With 2¾mm (No 12/US 2) needles, A
and right side facing, k up 16 sts down
left front neck, k centre front sts, k up
14 sts up right front neck, 8 sts down
right back neck, k centre back sts, k up
10 sts up left back neck.
110(114:122:130) sts.
K 1 row.

MEASUREMENTS

To fit age	6	12	24	36 months	
Actual chest measurement	60	68	76	87	cm
	23¾	26¾	30	34¼	in
Length	28	32	37	44	cm
	11	12½	14½	17¼	in
Sleeve seam	16	18	21	24	cm
	6¼	7	8¼	9½	in

Buttonhole row K2, k2tog, yf, k10, *skpo, k2tog, k27(29:33:37), skpo, k2tog*; k18, rep from * to *, k8.
K 1 row.
Next row K13, *skpo, k2tog, k25(27:31:35), skpo, k2tog*; k16, rep from * to *, k7.
K 1 row. Cast off knitwise, dec at corners as before.

TO MAKE UP
Lap left front shoulder over left back shoulder and catch side edges together. Sew on sleeves. Join sleeve seams, then side seams to top of side slits. Sew on buttons.

GARTER STITCH JACKET AND BOOTEES

MATERIALS
For the set 4(5:6) 25g balls of Jaeger Cashmere 4 ply.
Pair each of 3mm (No 11/US 2) and 3¼mm (No 10/US 3) knitting needles.
3 buttons.

TENSION
25 sts and 46 rows to 10cm/4in square over garter st (every row k) on 3¼mm (No 10/US 3) needles.

ABBREVIATIONS
See page 8.

JACKET
MAIN PART
Begin at lower edge of Back.
With 3¼mm (No 10/US 3) needles cast on 60(64:68) sts.
Work in garter st until Back measures 14(15:16)cm/5½(6:6¼)in from beg.
Shape Sleeves
Cast on 40(45:50) sts at beg of next 2 rows. 140(154:168) sts. Cont straight until back measures 24(26:28)cm/9½ (10¼:11)in from beg.
Divide for Fronts
Next row K55(61:67), cast off next 30(32:34) sts, k to end.
Work on last set of sts only for Left

MEASUREMENTS				
Jacket				
To fit age	**3**	**6**	**9 months**	
Actual chest measurement	48	51	54	cm
	19	20	21	in
Length	24	26	28	cm
	9½	10¼	11	in
Sleeve seam	12	14	16	cm
(with cuff turned back)	4¾	5½	6¼	in
Bootees				
To fit age	**0-9 months**			

Front.
Next row K.
Next row K2, m1, k to end.
Rep last 2 rows 8 times more. K 1 row.
Cast on 9(10:11) sts at beg of next row. 73(80:87) sts. Cont straight until work measures 34(37:40)cm/13½(14½: 15¾)in from beg, ending at outside edge.
Cast off 40(45:50) sts at beg of next row. 33(35:37) sts. Cont straight until work measures 48(52:56)cm/19(20½: 22)in from beg. Cast off.
Mark front edge of Left Front to indicate position of 3 buttons: first one 1cm/½in, second one 5(5.5:6)cm/2(2¼: 2½)in and third one 9(10:11)cm/3½ (4:4½)in up from cast on sts for neck.

Rejoin yarn at inside edge to rem sts for Right Front.
Next row K.
Next row K to last 2 sts, m1, k2.
Rep last 2 rows 8 times more. Cast on 9(10:11) sts at beg of next row. 73(80:87) sts. K 2 rows.
Buttonhole row (right side) K to last 4 sts, yf, k2tog, k2.
Complete as given for Left Front, making buttonholes at markers as before.

TO MAKE UP
Join side and underarm seams, reversing seams on last 4cm/1½in of underarm seams for cuffs. Turn back cuffs. Sew on buttons.

BOOTEES
TO MAKE

With 3mm (No 11/US 2) needles cast on 36 sts. K 21 rows.

Shape Instep

Next row K24, turn.

Next row K12, turn.

K 24 rows on this set of sts only.

Break off yarn.

With right side facing, rejoin yarn at base of instep and k up12 sts along side edge of instep, k across 12 sts of instep, k up 12 sts along other side of instep, k rem 12 sts. 60 sts. K 13 rows. Break off yarn.

Shape Sole

Next row With right side facing, sl first 24 sts onto right-hand needle, rejoin yarn and k12, turn.

Next row K11, k2tog, turn.

Rep last row 47 times more. 12 sts.

Next row [K2tog] to end. 6 sts.

Cast off.

Join back seam.

Make one more.

Garter Stitch Jacket illustrated overleaf

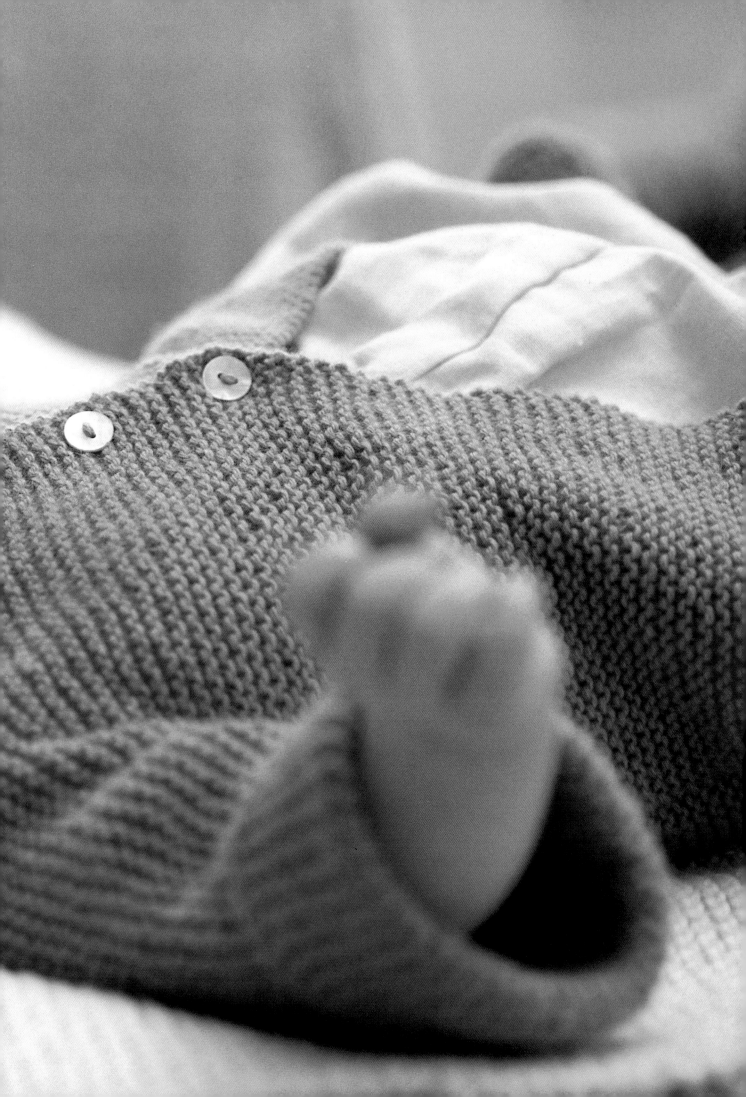

MOSS STITCH JACKET WITH COLLAR

MATERIALS

7(8:9:10) 50g balls of Rowan Cotton Glace.
Pair each of 2¾mm (No 12/US 2) and 3¼mm (No 10/US 3) knitting needles.
7(7:9:9) buttons.

TENSION

25 sts and 40 rows to 10cm/4in square over moss st on 3¼mm (No 10/US 3) needles.

ABBREVIATIONS

See page 8.

POCKET LININGS (make 2)

With 3¼mm (No 10/US 3) needles cast on 19(23:23:25) sts.
1st row K1, [p1, k1] to end.
This row forms moss st. Work a further 30(36:36:40) rows in moss st. Leave these sts on a holder.

RIGHT FRONT

With 3¼mm (No 10/US 3) needles cast on 53(57:59:63) sts.
Work 38(42:42:46) rows in moss st as given for Pocket Lining.
Place Pocket
Next row (right side) Moss st 24(24:24:26), cast off next 19(23:23:25) sts, moss st to end.
Next row Moss st 10(10:12:12), moss st across sts of Pocket Lining, moss st to end.
Work 8 rows in moss st.
***1st buttonholes row** Moss st 3, cast off 2, moss st 13(15:15:15) sts more, cast off 2, moss st to end.
2nd buttonholes row Moss st to end, casting on 2 sts over those cast off in previous row.
Moss st for a further 6(7.5:6:7)cm/2¼ (3:2¼:2¾)in, ending at front edge*. Rep from * to * 1(1:2:2) times more.
1st buttonhole row Moss st 3, cast off 2, moss st to end.

MEASUREMENTS

To fit age	6-12	12-18	18-24	24-36 months	
Actual chest measurement	65	70	74	79	cm
	25½	27½	29	31	in
Length	30	35	39	43	cm
	11¾	14	15¼	17	in
Sleeve seam	18	20	22	25	cm
(with cuff turned back)	7	8	8¾	10	in

2nd buttonhole row Moss st to end, casting on 2 sts over those cast off in previous row.
Moss st 2 rows. Work should measure 26(30:33.5:37.5)cm/10¼(12:13:14¾) in.
Shape Neck
Cast off 18 sts at beg of next row. Dec one st at neck edge on next 4(6:6:8) rows, then on 3 foll alt rows.
28(30:32:34) sts. Cont straight until Front measures 30(35:39:43)cm/11¾ (14:15¼:17)in from beg, ending with a right side row.
Shape Shoulder
Cast off 14(15:16:17) sts at beg of next row. Work 1 row. Cast off rem 14(15:16:17) sts.

LEFT FRONT

Work as given for Right Front, omitting buttonholes, reversing shapings and placing pocket as follows:
Next row (right side) Moss st 10(10:12:12), cast off next 19(23:23:25) sts, moss st to end.
Next row Moss st 24(24:24:26), moss st across sts of pocket lining, moss st to end.

BACK

With 3¼mm (No 10/US 3) needles cast on 81(87:93:99) sts.
Work in moss st as given for Pocket Lining until back measures same as Right Front to shoulder shaping, ending with a wrong side row.
Shape Shoulders
Cast off 14(15:16:17) sts at beg of next

4 rows. Cast off rem 25(27:29:31) sts.

SLEEVES

With 3¼mm (No 10/US 3) needles cast on 39(43:45:49) sts.
Work 20 rows in moss st as given for Pocket Lining for cuff.
Change to 2¾mm (No 12/US 2) needles.
Moss st 22 rows.
Change to 3¼mm (No 10/US 3) needles.
Cont in moss st and inc one st at each end of 3rd row and every foll 5th(5th:5th:6th) row until there are 55(61:67:71) sts. Cont straight until Sleeve measures 23(25:27:30)cm/9(10: 10¾:12)in from beg. Cast off.

COLLAR

Join shoulder seams.
With 2¾mm (No 12/US 2) needles, right side facing and beginning 11 sts away from right front edge, k up 24(27:28:28) sts up right front neck, 31(33:35:37) sts across back neck and 24(27:28:28) sts down left front neck, ending 11 sts away from front edge.
79(87:91:93) sts. Work 1 row in moss st as given for Pocket Lining.
Next 2 rows Moss st to last 23 sts, turn.
Next 2 rows Moss st to last 19 sts, turn.
Next 2 rows Moss st to last 15 sts, turn.
Next 2 rows Moss st to last 11 sts, turn.

Moss st to end. Moss st 5 rows across all sts.
Change to 3¼mm (No 10/US 3) needles.
Moss st 12 rows. Cast off in moss st.

BACK BELT
With 3¼mm (No 10/US 3) needles

cast on 59(65:71:77) sts.
Work 9 rows in moss st as given for Pocket Lining. Cast off in moss st.

TO MAKE UP
Catch down Pocket Linings. Sew on sleeves, placing centre of sleeves to

shoulder seams. Join side and sleeve seams, reversing seams on cuffs. Turn back cuffs. Sew on buttons. Place belt at desired position on Back and secure in place with buttons.

ANIMAL SLIPPERS

MATERIALS
Pig Two 50g balls of Rowan DK Handknit Cotton in Pink (A).
Oddment of Black for embroidery.
Pair each of 2¾mm (No 12/US 2) and 3¼mm (No 10/US 3) knitting needles.
Rabbit Two 50g balls of Rowan DK Handknit Cotton in Brown (A).
Small amounts of same in each of Pink and Cream.
Oddment of Black for embroidery.
Pair each of 2¾mm (No 12/US 2) and 3¼mm (No 10/US 3) knitting needles.
Sheep Two 50g balls of Rowan DK Handknit Cotton in Cream (A).
Small amount of same in Black.
Pair each of 2¾mm (No 12/US 2) and 3¼mm (No 10/US 3) knitting needles.

MEASUREMENTS
To fit age   **0-6 months**

ABBREVIATIONS
See page 8.

PIG SLIPPERS
MAIN PART
With 3¼mm (No 10/US 3) needles and A, cast on 22 sts. K 42 rows. Cast off.
Work two more pieces in same way.
Place two squares together and join around the edges, then fold three

corners into centre forming an open envelope. Join the two seams.
Fold remaining square diagonally to form triangle and join edges together.
Place joined edges of triangle to edges of open end of envelope, matching points. Sew in place.

SNOUT
With 3¼mm (No 10/US 3) needles and A, cast on 4 sts.
K 1 row. Cont in garter st (every row k), inc one st at each end of next 2 rows. 8 sts. K 8 rows. Dec one st at each end of next 2 rows. 4 sts. K 1 row. Cast off.
Make one more piece in same way.
Place pieces together and stitch all round, leaving an opening. Turn to right side and close opening. Sew to front of main part. With Black, embroider nostril.

EARS (make 2)
With 2¾mm (No 12/US 2) needles and A, cast on 5 sts.
Work 4 rows in garter st. Dec one st at each end of next row. Work 1 row.
K3tog and fasten off. Sew in place.

TAIL
With 2¾mm (No 12/US 2) needles and A, cast on 14 sts. Cast off. Run gathering thread along centre of tail.

Pull up slightly to form curl. Sew to back of main part.

RABBIT SLIPPERS
MAIN PART
Work as Main Part of Pig Slippers.

OUTER EARS (make 2)
With 3¼mm (No 10/US 3) needles and A, cast on 8 sts.
K 10 rows. Dec one st at each end of next row and foll 6th row. 4 sts. K 5 rows.
Next row [K2tog] twice.
K 1 row. K2tog and fasten off.

INNER EAR (make 2)
With 2¾mm (No 12/US 2) needles and Pink, cast on 8 sts.
K 10 rows. Dec one st at each end of next row and foll 6th row. 4 sts. K 5 rows.
Next row [K2tog] twice.
K 1 row. K2tog and fasten off.

TO MAKE UP
Sew inner ears to outer ears. Fold cast-on edge in half and stitch together folded edge. Sew ears in place. With Black, embroider nose. Make small pompon with Cream for tail and sew to back of main part.

SHEEP SLIPPERS
MAIN PART
Work as Main Part of Pig Slippers.
EARS (make 2)
With 2¾mm (No 12/US 2) needles and
Black, cast on 6 sts.
Work in garter st (every row k) for 4
rows. Dec one st at each end of next

row.
Next row [K2tog] twice.
K2tog and fasten off. Sew in place.
TAIL
With 2¾mm (No 12/US 2) needles and
Black, cast on 10 sts. Cast off.
Sew to back of main part.

FARMYARD BABY WRAP

MATERIALS

Six 50g balls of Rowan DK Handknit Cotton in Cream (A).
Small amounts of same in each of Pink, Brown, Blue and Yellow.
Pair each of 3¼mm (No 10/US 3) and 4mm (No 8/US 6) knitting needles.

MEASUREMENTS

Approximately
54cm x 63cm/21in x 25in.

TENSION

20 sts and 28 rows to 10cm/4in square over st st on 4mm (No 8/US 6) needles.

ABBREVIATIONS

See page 8.

NOTES

Read charts from right to left on right side rows and from left to right on wrong side rows. When working colour motifs, use separate lengths of contrast colour for each coloured area and twist yarns together on wrong side at joins to avoid holes.

TO MAKE

With 3¼mm (No 10/US 3) needles and A, cast on 109 sts.
1st row With A, k1, [p1, k1] to end. This row forms moss st. Rep last row 5 times more.
Change to 4mm (No 8/US 6) needles.
7th row (right side) With A, moss st 5, k 1st row of chart 1, with A, moss st 5, work 1st row of chart 2, with A, moss st 5, k 1st row of chart 3, with A, moss st 5, work 1st row of chart 4, with A, moss st 5.
8th row With A, moss st 5, work 2nd row of chart 4, with A, moss st 5, p 2nd row of chart 3, with A, moss st 5, work

2nd row of chart 2, with A, moss st 5, p 2nd row of chart 1, with A, moss st 5.
9th to 30th rows Rep last 2 rows 11 times more, working 3rd to 24th rows of charts.
31st to 36th rows As 1st row.
37th row With A, moss st 5, work 1st row of chart 5, with A, moss st 5, k 1st row of chart 6, with A, moss st 5, work 1st row of chart 2, with A, moss st 5, k 1st row of chart 7, with A, moss st 5.
38th row With A, moss st 5, p 2nd row of chart 7, with A, moss st 5, work 2nd row of chart 2, with A, moss st 5, p 2nd row of chart 6, with A, moss st 5, work 2nd row of chart 5, with A, moss st 5.
39th to 60th rows Rep last 2 rows 11 times more, working 3rd to 24th rows of charts.
61st to 66th rows As 1st row.
67th row With A, moss st 5, k 1st row of chart 8, with A, moss st 5, work 1st row of chart 4, with A, moss st 5, k 1st row of chart 9, with A, moss st 5, work 1st row of chart 2, with A, moss st 5.
68th row With A, moss st 5, work 2nd row of chart 2, with A, moss st 5, p 2nd row of chart 9, with A, moss st 5, work 2nd row of chart 4, with A, moss st 5, p 2nd row of chart 8, with A, moss st 5.
69th to 90th rows Rep last 2 rows 11 times more, working 3rd to 24th rows of charts.
91st to 96th rows As 1st row.
97th row With A, moss st 5, work 1st row of chart 2, with A, moss st 5, k 1st row of chart 1, with A, moss st 5, work 1st row of chart 10, with A, moss st 5, k 1st row of chart 3, with A, moss st 5.
98th row With A, moss st 5, p 2nd row of chart 3, with A, moss st 5, work 2nd row of chart 10, with A, moss st 5, p 2nd row of chart 1, with A, moss st 5, work 2nd row of chart 2, with A, moss st 5.
99th to 120th rows Rep last 2 rows

11 times more, working 3rd to 24th rows of charts.
121st to 126th rows As 1st row.
127th row With A, moss st 5, k 1st row of chart 11, with A, moss st 5, work 1st row of chart 2, with A, moss st 5, k 1st row of chart 6, with A, moss st 5, work 1st row of chart 4, with A, moss st 5.
128th row With A, moss st 5, work 2nd row of chart 4, with A, moss st 5, p 2nd row of chart 6, with A, moss st 5, work 2nd row of chart 2, with A, moss st 5, p 2nd row of chart 11, with A, moss st 5.
129th to 150th rows Rep last 2 rows 11 times more, working 3rd to 24th rows of charts.
151st to 156th rows As 1st row.
157th row With A, moss st 5, work 1st row of chart 10, with A, moss st 5, k 1st row of chart 8, with A, moss st 5, work 1st row of chart 2, with A, moss st 5, k 1st row of chart 9, with A, moss st 5.
158th row With A, moss st 5, p 2nd row of chart 9, with A, moss st 5, work 2nd row of chart 2, with A, moss st 5, p 2nd row of chart 8, with A, moss st 5, work 2nd row of chart 10, with A, moss st 5.
159th to 180th rows Rep last 2 rows 11 times more, working 3rd to 24th rows of charts.
Change to 3¼mm (No 10/US 3) needles.
Rep 1st row 6 times. Cast off in moss st.
With Pink and back stitch, embroider pigs' tails and with Brown, embroider their eyes. Outline the bodies of cows and sheep with Brown, using back stitch. With Yellow, work a few straight stitches for scarecrow's hands and embroider hen's legs and beak. Work few straight stitches with Pink for hen's tail and lazy daisy stitch for its wattle.

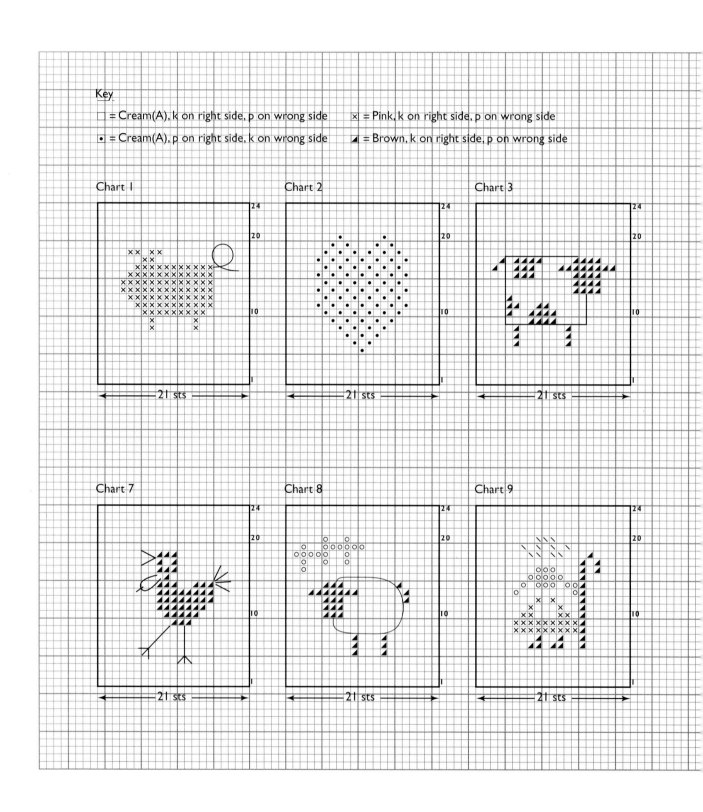

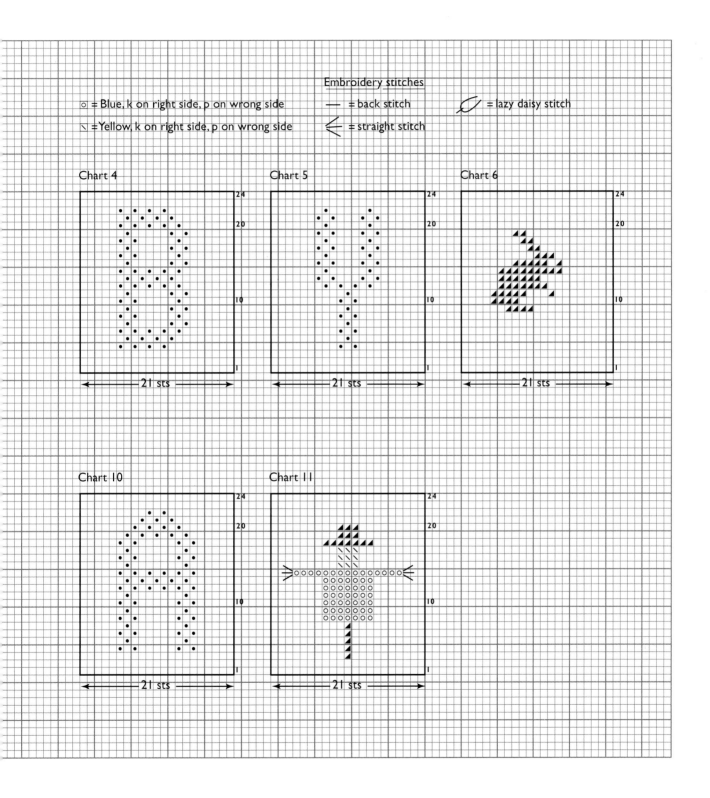

Embroidery stitches

⊙ = Blue, k on right side, p on wrong side   — = back stitch   ⬭ = lazy daisy stitch

◩ = Yellow, k on right side, p on wrong side   ⟨ = straight stitch

Chart 4

Chart 5

Chart 6

Chart 10

Chart 11

Fair isle twinset

MATERIALS

Cardigan 4(5:6) 50g balls of Rowan Cotton Glace in Oyster (A).
1 ball of same in each of Blue, Cream, Red, Yellow and Green.
Pair each of 2¾mm (No 12/US 2) and 3¼mm (No 10/US 3) knitting needles.
6(7:8) buttons.
Jumper 3(3:4) 50g balls of Rowan Cotton Glace in Oyster (A).
Small amount of same in each of Blue, Cream, Red, Yellow and Green.
Pair each of 2¾mm (No 12/US 2) and 3¼mm (No 10/US 3) knitting needles.
3 buttons.

TENSION

25 sts and 34 rows to 10cm/4in square over st st on 3¼mm (No 10/US 3) needles.

ABBREVIATIONS

See page 8.

NOTE

Read chart from right to left on right side rows and from left to right on wrong side rows. When working in pattern, strand yarn not in use loosely across wrong side to keep fabric elastic.

CARDIGAN
BACK AND FRONTS

Knitted in one piece to armholes.
With 2¾mm (No 12/US 2) needles and A, cast on 157(173:189) sts.
1st rib row (right side) K2, [p1, k1] to last 3 sts, p1, k2.
2nd rib row K1, [p1, k1] to end.
Rep last 2 rows once more.
Buttonhole row Rib 3, yrn, p2tog, rib to end.
Rib 6 rows more.
Next row Rib 6 and slip these 6 sts onto a safety pin, rib to last 6 sts and slip the last 6 sts onto a safety pin. 145(161:177) sts.
Change to 3¼mm (No 10/US 3) needles.
Beg with a k row, work 4(6:8) rows in st st. Cont in st st and patt from chart until 13th row of chart has been worked. Cont in A only until work measures 13(16:20)cm/5(6¼:8)in from beg, ending with a p row.
Right Front
Next row K36(40:44), turn.
Work on this set of sts only.

MEASUREMENTS

To fit age	6-12	12-18	24-36 months	
Cardigan				
Actual chest measurement	59	65	72	cm
	23¼	25½	28½	in
Length	25	30	35	cm
	10	11¾	13¾	in
Sleeve seam	20	23	26	cm
	8	9	10¼	in
Jumper				
Actual chest measurement	52	58	65	cm
	20½	22¾	25½	in
Length	23	28	34	cm
	9	11	13½	in
Sleeve seam	6	7	8	cm
	2½	2¾	3	in

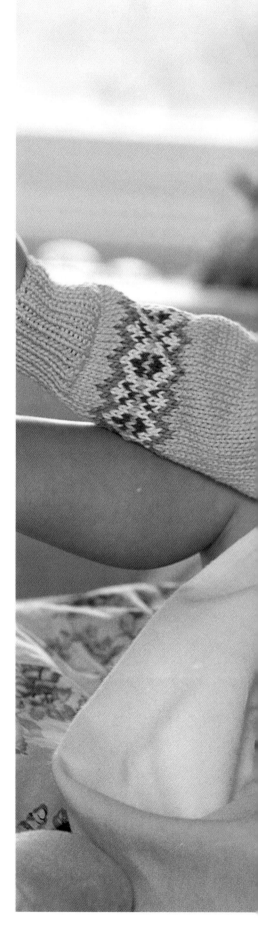

Shape Armhole

P 1 row.

Next row K to last 3 sts, k2tog, k1.
Rep last 2 rows 4(5:6) times more.
31(34:37) sts. Cont straight until work
measures 21(25:30)cm/8¼(9¾:11¾)in
from beg, ending with a p row.

Shape Neck

Next row K5(6:7) and slip these sts
onto a safety pin, k to end.

Next row P to last 3 sts, p2tog tbl, p1.

Next row K1, skpo, k to end.
Rep last 2 rows 3 times more.
18(20:22) sts. Cont straight until work
measures 25(30:35)cm/10(11¾:13¾)in
from beg, ending at armhole edge.

Shape Shoulder

Cast off 9(10:11) sts at beg of next
row. Work 1 row. Cast off rem 9(10:11)
sts.

Back

With right side facing, rejoin yarn to
rem sts, k73(81:89), turn.

Shape Armholes

P 1 row.

Next row K1, skpo, k to last 3 sts,
k2tog, k1.
Rep last 2 rows 4(5:6) times more.
63(69:75) sts. Cont straight until Back
measures same as Right Front to
shoulder shaping, ending with a p row.

Shape Shoulders

Cast off 9(10:11) sts at beg of next 4
rows. Leave rem 27(29:31) sts on a
holder.

Left Front

With right side facing, rejoin yarn to
rem sts and k to end.

Shape Armhole

P 1 row.

Next row K1, skpo, k to end.
Rep last 2 rows 4(5:6) times more.
31(34:37) sts. Cont straight until work
measures same as Right Front to neck
shaping, ending with a k row.

Shape Neck

Next row P5(6:7) and slip these sts
onto a safety pin, p to end.

Next row K to last 3 sts, k2tog, k1.

Next row P1, p2tog, p to end.

Complete as given for Right Front.

SLEEVES

With 2¾mm (No 12/US 2) needles and
A, cast on 42(46:50) sts.
Work 14(16:18) rows in k1, p1 rib, inc
one st at centre of last row.
43(47:51) sts.
Change to 3¼mm (No 10/US 3)
needles.
Beg with a k row, work 4 rows in st st,
inc one st at each end of 3rd row.
45(49:53) sts. Work 13 rows of patt
from chart, **at the same time**, inc
one st at each end of 3rd row and 2
foll 4th rows, working inc sts into patt.
51(55:59) sts. Cont in A only, inc one st
at each end of 2nd row and every foll
4th row until there are 65(71:77) sts.
Cont straight until sleeve measures
20(23:26)cm/8(9:10¼)in from beg,
ending with a p row.

Shape Top

Next row K1, skpo, k to last 3 sts,
k2tog, k1.
P 1 row. Rep last 2 rows 4(5:6) times
more. 55(59:63) sts. Cast off.

BUTTON BAND

With 2¾mm (No 12/US 2) needles,
rejoin A yarn at inside edge to the 6
sts of Left Front welt, cast on 1 st, rib
to end. Cont in rib until band when
slighty stretched fits along front edge to
neck edge, ending at inside edge. Leave
these sts on a safety pin. Sew band in
place. Mark position for 6(7:8) buttons:
first one to match buttonhole already
made on Right Front, last one to be
worked on 4th row of neckband and
rem 4(5:6) evenly spaced between.

BUTTONHOLE BAND

Work to match Button Band, making
buttonholes at markers as before and
ending at outside edge. Leave sts on
needle. Sew band in place.

NECKBAND

Join shoulder seams.

With 2¾mm (No 12/US 2) needles, A
and right side facing, rib first 6 sts of
buttonhole band, work last st tog with
first st of neck shaping, k rem 4(5:6) sts,
pick up and k 14 sts up right front
neck, k back neck sts, pick up and k14
sts down left front neck, k first 4(5:6)
sts of neck shaping, work last st tog
with first st of button band, rib rem 6
sts. 77(81:85) sts. Rib 7 rows, making
buttonhole on 4th row as before. Cast
off in rib.

TO MAKE UP

Sew on sleeves. Join sleeve seams. Sew
on buttons.

JUMPER
BACK

With 2¾mm (No 12/US 2) needles and
A, cast on 65(73:81) sts.

1st rib row (right side) K1, [p1, k1]
to end.

2nd rib row P1, [k1, p1] to end.
Rib 10 rows more.
Change to 3¼mm (No 10/US 3)
needles.
Beg with a k row, work in st st until
back measures 13(16:20)cm/5(6¼:8)in
from beg, ending with a p row.

Shape Armholes

Next row K1, skpo, k to last 3 sts,
k2tog, k1.
P 1 row. Rep last 2 rows twice more,
then work first of the 2 rows again.
57(65:73) sts. Work 1(5:9) rows
straight. Work in patt from chart until
13th row of chart has been worked.
Cont in A only, work 3 rows.**

Divide for Opening

Next row K26(30:34), turn.
Work on this set of sts only until Back
measures 23(28:34)cm/9(11:13½)in
from beg, ending at armhole edge.

Shape Shoulder

Cast off 9(10:11) sts at beg of next
row and foll alt row. Leave rem
8(10:12) sts on a holder.
With right side facing, slip centre 5 sts
onto a safety pin, rejoin yarn to rem sts

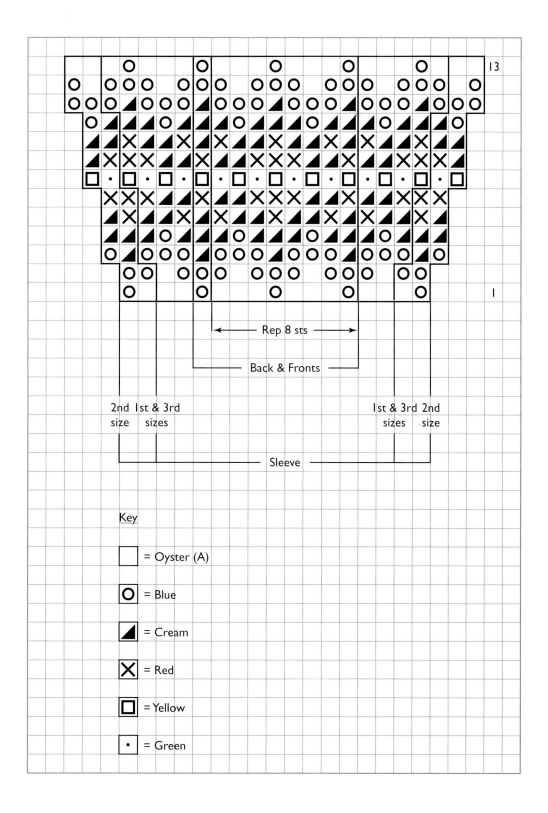

Key

☐ = Oyster (A)

Ⓞ = Blue

◢ = Cream

☒ = Red

⊡ = Yellow

• = Green

and k to end. Complete as given for first side.

FRONT

Work as given for Back to **.

Shape Neck

Next row K21(24:27), turn.
Work on this set of sts only.
Next row P1, p2tog, p to end.
Next row K to last 3 sts, k2tog, k1.
Dec at neck edge as set on next 1(2:3) rows. 18(20:22) sts. Cont straight until Front matches Back to shoulder shaping, ending at armhole edge.

Shape Shoulder

Cast off 9(10:11) sts at beg of next row. Work 1 row. Cast off rem 9(10:11) sts.
With right side facing, slip centre 15(17:19) sts onto a holder, rejoin yarn to rem sts, k to end.
Next row P to last 3 sts, p2tog tbl, p1.
Next row K1, skpo, k to end.
Complete as given for first side.

SLEEVES

With 2¾mm (No 12/US 2) needles and A, cast on 52(56:60) sts.
Work 4 rows in k1, p1 rib.

Change to 3¼mm (No 10/US 3) needles.
Beg with a k row, work in st st, inc one st at each end of 3rd row and 2(3:4) foll 4th rows. 58(64:70) sts. Work 5 rows straight.

Shape Top

Next row K1, skpo, k to last 3 sts, k2tog, k1.
P 1 row. Rep last 2 rows 3 times more. 50(56:62) sts. Cast off.

BUTTON BAND

With 2¾mm (No 12/US 2) needles and A, cast on 7 sts.
1st rib row (right side) K2, p1, k1, p1, k2.
2nd rib row K1, [p1, k1] 3 times.
Rep last 2 rows 6(7:8) times more.
Leave these sts on a safety pin.

BUTTONHOLE BAND

With 2¾mm (No 12/US 2) needles and right side facing, rejoin A yarn to sts at base of back opening, k2, m1, k2, k twice in next st. 7 sts.
1st rib row (wrong side) K1, [p1, k1] 3 times.
2nd rib row K2, p1, k1, p1, k2.

Rib 1(3:5) rows more.
Buttonhole row Rib 3, yrn , p2tog, rib 2.
Rib 5 rows. Work the buttonhole row again. Rib 3 rows more. Leave sts on needle.

NECKBAND

Join shoulder seams. Sew on buttonhole band to left side edge of opening and button band to right side edge. Catch down cast on sts of Button Band on wrong side at base of opening. With 2¾mm (No 12/US 2) needles, right side facing and A, rib the 6 sts of buttonhole band, work last st tog with first st of back neck sts, k rem 7(9:11) sts, pick up and k12(14:15) sts down left front neck, k centre front sts, pick up and k12(14:15) sts up right front neck, k first 7(9:11) sts of back neck, work last st tog with first st of button band, rib rem 6 sts. 67(77:85) sts. Work 7 rows in rib, making buttonhole on 2nd row as before. Cast off in rib.

TO MAKE UP

Sew on sleeves. Join side and sleeve seams. Sew on buttons.

TWO-COLOUR JACKET WITH ZIP

MATERIALS

5(6) 50g balls of Rowan DK Handknit Cotton in Navy (A).
1 ball of same in Cream (B).
Pair each of 3¼mm (No 10/US 3) and 4mm (No 8/US 6) knitting needles.
25(30)cm/10(12)in open-ended zip.

MEASUREMENTS

To fit age	6-12	12-24 months	
Actual chest measurement	64	76	cm
	25	30	in
Length	33	37	cm
	13	14½	in
Sleeve seam	20	23	cm
	8	9	in

TENSION

20 sts and 28 rows to 10cm/4in square over st st on 4mm (No 8/US 6) needles.

ABBREVIATIONS

See page 8.

NOTES

Read charts from right to left on right side rows and from left to right on wrong side rows. When working in pattern, strand yarn not in use loosely across wrong side to keep fabric elastic.

BACK AND FRONTS

Knitted in one piece to armholes.

With 3¼mm (No 10/US 3) needles and A, cast on 129(153) sts.

Next row K1, [p1, k1] to end.

This row forms moss st. Moss st 5 rows more.

Change to 4mm (No 8/US 6) needles.

Next row (right side) Moss st 3, k to last 3 sts, moss st 3.

Next row Moss st 3, p to last 3 sts, moss st 3.

Using separate small balls of A yarn at each end and twisting yarns together on wrong side at joins to avoid holes, work as follows:

Next row With A, moss st 3, k 1 edge st of 1st row of chart 1, k across 6 st patt rep 20(24) times, k 2 edge sts, with A, moss st 3.

Next row With A, moss st 3, p 2 edge sts of 2nd row of chart 1, p across 6 st patt rep 20(24) times, p 1 edge st, with A, moss st 3.

Work a further 15 rows as set.

Keeping the 3 sts at front edge in moss st and remainder in st st, cont in A only until work measures 20(22)cm/8(8¾)in from beg, ending with a wrong side row.

Right Front

Next row Moss st 3, k29(35), turn. Work on this set of sts only. Work 1 row.

Next row With A, moss st 3, k 1st row of chart 2 to end.

Next row P 2nd row of chart 2 to last 3 sts, with A, moss st 3.

Work as set until front measures 27(31)cm/10¾(12¼)in from beg, ending at front edge.

Shape Neck

Next row Moss st 3 and slip these 3 sts onto safety pin, patt to end.

Keeping patt correct, dec one st at neck edge on every row until 20(24) sts rem. Cont straight until front measures 33(37)cm/13(14½)in from beg, ending at armhole edge.

Shape Shoulder

Cast off 10(12) sts at beg of next row. Work 1 row. Cast off rem 10(12) sts.

Back

With right side facing, rejoin A yarn to rem sts, k65(77), turn. P 1 row.

Work in patt from chart 2 until Back measures same as Right Front to shoulder shaping, ending with a wrong side row.

Shape Shoulders

Cast off 10(12) sts at beg of next 4 rows. Cast off rem 25(29) sts.

Left Front

With right side facing, rejoin A yarn to rem sts, k to last 3 sts, moss st 3. Work 1 row.

Next row K across 1st row of chart 2 to last 3 sts, with A, moss st 3.

Next row With A, moss st 3, p across 2nd row of chart 2 to end.

Complete as given for Right Front.

SLEEVES

With 3¼mm (No 10/US 3) needles

and A, cast on 33(39) sts.

Work 6 rows in moss st.

Change to 4mm (No 8/US 6) needles.

Beg with a k row, work 2 rows in st st.

Work the 17 rows of chart 1, **at the same time**, inc one st at each end of 3rd row and 3 foll 4th rows, working inc sts into patt. 41(47) sts. Cont in A only, inc one st at each end of 2nd row and every foll 4th row until there are 53(61) sts. Cont straight until sleeve measures 20(23)cm/8(9)in from beg, ending with a p row. Cast off.

COLLAR

With 3¼mm (No 10/US 3) needles, rejoin A yarn at inside edge to the 3 sts on right front safety pin. Cont in moss st, inc one st at inside edge on next 11(15) rows, then on every foll alt row until there are 21(25) sts, ending at outside edge.

Next 2 rows Moss st 11(13), turn, sl 1, moss st to end.

Moss st 4 rows. Rep last 6 rows 6(7) times more. Cast off.

Work left side of collar as given for right side.

TO MAKE UP

Join shoulder seams.

Join back seam of collar and sew collar in position. Sew in sleeves, placing centre of sleeves to shoulder seams. Join sleeve seams. Sew in zip. With B, work single cross stitch along welts, cuffs and outside edge of collar. Embroider single cross stitch between pattern on first and last 3 rows of chart 1 pattern and on 1st to 3rd and 15th to 17th rows of chart 2 pattern on back, fronts and sleeves.

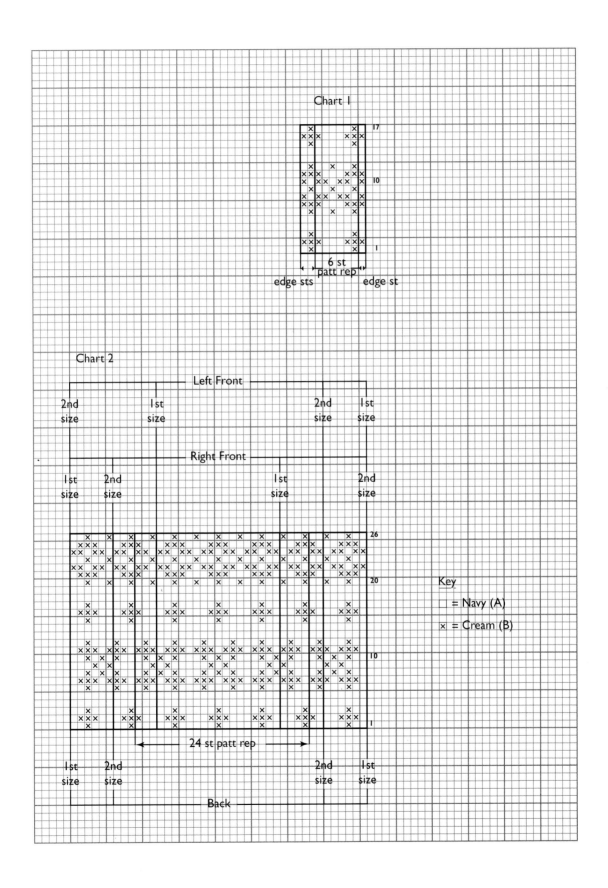

Chart 1

17

10

1

6 st
patt rep

edge sts   edge st

Chart 2

Left Front

| 2nd | 1st | | 2nd | 1st |
| size | size | | size | size |

Right Front

| 1st | 2nd | | 1st | 2nd |
| size | size | | size | size |

26

20

Key

☐ = Navy (A)

☒ = Cream (B)

10

1

← 24 st patt rep →

| 1st | 2nd | | 2nd | 1st |
| size | size | | size | size |

Back

BASKET-WEAVE JACKET

MATERIALS

Four 100g hanks of Rowan Magpie.
Pair each of 4½mm (No 7/US 7) and
5mm (No 6/US 8) knitting needles.
4 buttons.

MEASUREMENTS

To fit age	2	3 years	
Actual chest	63	72	cm
measurement	24¾	28½	in
Length	35	40	cm
	13¾	15¾	in
Sleeve seam	20	24	cm
	8	9½	in

TENSION

17 sts and 28 rows to 10cm/4in square
over pattern on 5mm (No 6/US 8)
needles.

ABBREVIATIONS

See page 8.

BACK

With 4½mm (No 7/US 7) needles cast
on 54(62) sts.
K 5 rows.
Change to 5mm (No 6/US 8) needles.
1st row (right side) K5, [p4, k4] to
last 9 sts, p4, k5.
2nd row P.
3rd and 4th rows As 1st and 2nd
rows.
5th row As 1st row.
6th row K5, [p4, k4] to last 9 sts, p4,
k5.
7th row K.
8th and 9th rows As 6th and 7th
rows.
10th row As 6th row.
These 10 rows form patt. Cont in patt
until Back measures approximately
35(40)cm/13¾(15¾)in from beg, ending
with 10th(6th) patt row.

Shape Shoulders

Cast off 15(18) sts at beg of next 2
rows. Cast off rem 24(26) sts.

POCKET LININGS (make 2)

With 5mm (No 6/US 8) needles cast
on 16(20) sts.
1st row P2(4), k4, p4, k4, p2(4).
2nd row P.
3rd and 4th rows As 1st and 2nd
rows.
5th row As 1st row.
6th row P2(4), k4, p4, k4, p2(4).
7th row K.
8th and 9th rows As 6th and 7th
rows.
10th row As 6th row.
These 10 rows form patt. Patt a further
10(16) rows. Leave these sts on a
holder.

LEFT FRONT

With 4½mm (No 7/US 7) needles cast
on 29(33) sts.
K 5 rows.
Change to 5mm (No 6/US 8) needles.
1st row (right side) P5, [k4, p4] to
last 8(4) sts, k8(4).
2nd row K4, p to end.
3rd and 4th rows As 1st and 2nd
rows.
5th row As 1st row.
6th row K8(4), [p4, k4] to last 5 sts,
p5.
7th row K.
8th and 9th rows As 6th and 7th
rows.
10th row As 6th row.
These 10 rows form patt. Patt a further
20(26) rows.

Place Pocket

Next row Patt 3(1), slip next 16(20)
sts onto a holder, patt across sts of
pocket lining, patt to end.
Cont in patt until work measures
22(25)cm/8¾(9¾)in from beg, ending at
side edge.

Shape Neck

Next row Patt to last 4 sts, slip these
4 sts onto safety pin.
Keeping patt correct, dec one st at

neck edge on next 5 alt rows, then on
every foll 4th row until 15(18) sts rem.
Cont straight until Front matches Back
to shoulder shaping, ending at side
edge. Cast off.
Mark front edge to indicate buttons:
first one to come 5 rows up from
lower edge, last one 3 rows below
neck shaping and rem 2 evenly spaced
between.

RIGHT FRONT

With 4½mm (No 7/US 7) needles cast
on 29(33) sts.
K 5 rows.
Change to 5mm (No 6/US 8) needles.
1st (buttonhole) row (right side)
K1, k2tog, yf, k5(1), [p4, k4] to last 5 sts,
p5.
2nd row P to last 4 sts, k4.
3rd row K8(4), [p4, k4] to last 5 sts,
p5.
4th and 5th rows As 2nd and 3rd
rows.
6th row P5, [k4, p4] to last 8(4) sts,
k8(4).
7th row K.
8th and 9th rows As 6th and 7th
rows.
10th row As 6th row.
These 10 rows set the patt.
Patt a further 20(26) rows, making
buttonhole to match marker on Left
Front as before.

Place Pocket

Next row Patt 10(12), slip next
16(20) sts onto a holder, patt across sts
of pocket lining, patt 3(1).
Complete as given for Left Front,
making buttonholes at markers as
before.

RIGHT SLEEVE

With 4½mm (No 7/US 7) needles cast
on 28(32) sts.
K 5 rows.
Change to 5mm (No 6/US 8) needles.

1st row (right side) P2(0), [k4, p4] to last 2(0) sts, k2(0).

2nd row P.

These 2 rows set the patt. Cont in patt to match Back, inc one st at each end of 5th row and every foll 4th row until there are 48(56) sts, working inc sts into patt. Cont straight until sleeve measures approximately 20(24)cm/8 (9½)in from beg, ending with 10th patt row. Cast off.

LEFT SLEEVE

With 4½mm (No 7/US 7) needles cast on 28(32) sts.
K 5 rows.
Change to 5mm (No 6/US 8) needles.
1st row (right side) K2(0), [p4, k4] to last 2(0) sts, p2(0).

2nd row P.

These 2 rows set the patt. Complete as given for Right Sleeve.

COLLAR

Join shoulder seams.
With 4½mm (No 7/US 7) needles, rejoin yarn at inside edge to the 4 sts on right front safety pin, k4. Work in garter st (every row k), inc one st at inside edge on next row and every foll alt row until there are 21(25) sts. Cont straight until shaped edge of collar fits along shaped edge of Front to shoulder seam, ending at outside edge.
Next 2 rows K12(14), turn, sl 1, k to end.
K 7 rows.
Rep last 8 rows 2(3) times more, then

work the 2 turning rows again. K 2 rows. Cast off.
Work left side of collar as given for right side.

POCKET TOPS

With 4½mm (No 7/US 7) needles and right side facing, k across sts of pocket top. K 4 rows. Cast off.

TO MAKE UP

Catch down pocket linings and sides of pocket tops. Join back seam of collar and sew collar in place. Placing centre of sleeves to shoulder seams, sew on sleeves, matching pattern. Join side and sleeve seams. Sew on buttons.

CABLE AND RIB TUNIC

MATERIALS

7(8:9) 50g balls of Rowan DK Handknit Cotton.
Pair each of 3¾mm (No 9/US 4) and 4mm (No 8/US 6) knitting needles.
Set of four 3¾mm (No 9/US 4) double-pointed knitting needles.
Cable needle.

TENSION

23 sts and 29 rows to 10cm/4in square over rib, when slightly stretched on 4mm (No 8/US 6) needles.

ABBREVIATIONS

C8B = sl next 4 sts onto cable needle and leave at back of work, k4, then k4 from cable needle;
C8F = sl next 4 sts onto cable needle and leave at front of work, k4, then k4 from cable needle.
Also see page 8.

MEASUREMENTS

To fit age	1	2	3 years	
Actual chest measurement	62	71	80	cm
	24½	28	31½	in
Length	30	34	38	cm
	11¾	13½	15	in
Sleeve seam	19	21	23	cm
	7½	8¼	9	in

BACK AND FRONT (alike)

With 3¾mm (No 9/US 4) needles cast on 72(82:92) sts.
1st row (right side) P2, [k3, p2] 6(7:8) times, k8, p2, [k3, p2] 6(7:8) times.
2nd row K2, [p3, k2] 6(7:8) times, p8, k2, [p3, k2] 6(7:8) times.
Rep last 2 rows once more.
Inc row P2, [k3, p2] 6(7:8) times, k1, [m1, k2] 3 times, m1, k1, p2, [k3, p2] 6(7:8) times. 76(86:96) sts.
Change to 4mm (No 8/US 6) needles.

1st row (wrong side) K2, [p3, k2] 6(7:8) times, p12, k2, [p3, k2] 6(7:8) times.
2nd row P2, [k3, p2] 6(7:8) times, k4, C8B, p2, [k3, p2] 6(7:8) times.
3rd row As 1st row.
4th row P2, [k3, p2] 6(7:8) times, k12, p2, [k3, p2] 6(7:8) times.
5th row As 1st row.
6th row P2, [k3, p2] 6(7:8) times, C8F, k4, p2, [k3, p2] 6(7:8) times.
7th row As 1st row.
8th row As 4th row.

These 8 rows form patt. Cont in patt until back measures 26(30:34)cm/10¼ (12:13½)in from beg, ending with wrong side row.

Shape Shoulders

Cast off 28(32:36) sts at beg of next 2 rows. Leave rem 20(22:24) sts on a holder.

SLEEVES

With 3¾mm (No 9/US 4) needles cast on 42(46:52) sts.

1st row (right side) K0(2:0), p2, [k3, p2] 3(3:4) times, k8, p2, [k3, p2] 3(3:4) times, k0(2:0).

2nd row P0(2:0), k2, [p3, k2] 3(3:4) times, p8, k2, [p3, k2] 3(3:4) times, p0(2:0).

Rep last 2 rows once more.

Inc row K0(2:0), p2, [k3, p2] 3(3:4) times, k1, [m1, k2] 3 times, m1, k1, p2, [k3, p2] 3(3:4) times, k0(2:0). 46(50:56) sts.

Change to 4mm (No 8/US 6) needles.

1st row (wrong side) P0(2:0), k2, [p3, k2] 3(3:4) times, p12, k2, [p3, k2] 3(3:4) times, p0(2:0).

2nd row K0(2:0), p2, [k3, p2] 3(3:4) times, k4, C8B, p2, [k3, p2] 3(3:4) times, k0(2:0).

3rd row As 1st row.

4th row K0(2:0), p2, [k3, p2] 3(3:4) times, k12, p2, [k3, p2] 3(3:4) times, k0(2:0).

5th row As 1st row.

6th row K0(2:0), p2, [k3, p2] 3(3:4) times, C8F, k4, p2, [k3, p2] 3(3:4) times, k0(2:0).

7th row As 1st row.

8th row As 4th row.

These 8 rows form patt. Cont in patt, inc one st at each end of 2nd row, 5 foll 2nd(3rd:3rd) rows then on every foll 3rd(3rd:4th) row until there are 72(76:82) sts, working inc sts into rib. Cont straight until sleeve measures 19(21:23)cm/7½(8¼:9)in from beg, ending with a wrong side row.

Shape Saddle Shoulder

Cast off 24(26:29) sts at beg of next 2 rows. 24 sts.

Work 18(22:26) rows straight.

Shape Neck

Next row Patt 6, turn.

Work on this set of sts only. Dec one st at inside (neck) edge on next row and 3 foll alt rows. Patt 1 row. Work 2tog and fasten off.

With right side facing, slip centre 12 sts onto a holder, rejoin yarn to rem sts and patt to end. Complete as given for first side.

COLLAR

Join both front and back saddle shoulder seams.

With set of four 3¾mm (No 9/US 4) needles and right side facing, slip first 10(11:12) sts at centre front onto a holder, join in yarn and [k2tog] twice, k6(7:8) across rem sts, k up 8 sts along shaped edge of right sleeve, [k2tog] 6 times across centre sleeve sts, k up 8 sts up other side of shaped edge of sleeve, k6(7:8), [k2tog] 4 times, k6(7:8) across back neck sts, k up 8 sts along shaped edge of left sleeve, [k2tog] 6 times across centre sleeve sts, k up 8 sts up other side of shaped edge of sleeve, k6(7:8), [k2tog] twice across sts on front holder. 76(80:84) sts. Work in rounds as follows:

1st rib round K1, [p2, k2] to last 3 sts, p2, k1.

Rep last round 5 times more.

Next round K1, [p1, m1, p1, k2] to last 3 sts, p1, m1, p1, k1, turn. 95(100:105) sts.

Work in rows as follows:

Next row K4, [p2, k3] to last 6 sts, p2, k4.

Next row K1, p3, [k2, p3] to last st, k1.

Rep last 2 rows 6(7:8) times more.

Cast off in rib.

TO MAKE UP

Sew on remainder of sleeves in place. Join side and sleeve seams.

SWEATER WITH HOOD

MATERIALS

5(6:7:8) 50g balls of Rowan Designer DK Wool.

Pair each of 3¾mm (No 9/US 4) and 4mm (No 8/US 6) knitting needles.

One 3¾mm (No 9/US 4) circular knitting needle.

MEASUREMENTS

To fit age	6	12	24	36 months	
Actual chest measurement	58	62	72	82	cm
	23	24½	28½	32¼	in
Length	28	32	37	42	cm
	11	12½	14½	16½	in
Sleeve seam	17	20	22	24	cm
(with cuff turned back)	6¾	8	8¾	9½	in

TENSION

24 sts and 36 rows to 10cm/4in square over double moss stitch on 4mm (No 8/US 6) needles.

ABBREVIATIONS

See page 8

BACK

With 3¾mm (No 9/US 4) needles cast on 70(74:86:98) sts.

1st rib row (right side) K4, [p2, k2] to last 6 sts, p2, k4.

2nd rib row K2, [p2, k2] to end.

Rep last 2 rows 7 times more.

Change to 4mm (No 8/US 6) needles.

1st row K2, [p2, k2] to end.

2nd row P2, [k2, p2] to end.

3rd row P2, [k2, p2] to end.

4th row K2, [p2, k2] to end.

These 4 rows form double moss st patt. Cont in patt until work measures 28(32:37:42)cm/11(12½:14½:16½)in from beg, ending with a wrong side row.

Shape Shoulders

Cast off 18(19:23:27) sts at beg of next 2 rows. Cast off rem 34(36:40:44) sts.

FRONT

Work as given for Back until Front measures 17(20:23:26)cm/6¾(8:9:10¼)in from beg, ending with a right side row.

Shape Opening

Next row Patt 27(28:33:37), cast off next 16(18:20:24) sts, patt to end.

Work on last set of 27(28:33:37) sts for left side of front neck until Front matches Back to shoulder shaping, ending at side edge.

Shape Shoulder

Next row Cast off 18(19:23:27) sts, patt to end.

Patt 1 row on rem 9(9:10:10) sts. Leave these sts on a holder.

With right side facing, rejoin yarn to rem sts, patt to end. Cont until Front matches Back to shoulder shaping, ending at side edge.

Shape Shoulder

Next row Cast off 18(19:23:27) sts, patt to end.

Leave rem 9(9:10:10) sts on a holder.

SLEEVES

With 4mm (No 8/US 6) needles cast on 42(46:50:54) sts.

1st rib row K2, [p2, k2] to end.

2nd rib row P2, [k2, p2] to end.

Rep these 2 rows 7 times more.

Change to 3¾mm (No 9/US 4) needles.

Rib 20 rows more.

Change to 4mm (No 8/US 6) needles.

Work in double moss st patt as given for Back, inc one st at each end of 3rd row and every foll 4th row until there are 58(66:74:82) sts, working inc sts into patt. Cont straight until work measures 22(25:27:29)cm/8¾(10:10¾:11½)in from beg, ending with a wrong side row. Cast off in patt.

HOOD

Join shoulder seams.

With 4mm (No 8/US 6) needles and right side facing, patt across 9(9:10:10) sts on right front neck holder, k up 34(36:40:44) sts across back neck, patt 9(9:10:10) sts on left front neck holder. 52(54:60:64) sts.

Next row Patt 10(9:10:10), [k twice in next st] 32(36:40:44) times, patt to end. 84(90:100:108) sts.

Work in patt across all sts for a further 19(20:21:22)cm/7½(8:8¼:8¾)in, ending with a wrong side row.

Shape Top

Next row Patt 42(45:50:54), turn.

Work on this set of sts only. Cast off 6 sts at beg of next row and 4(4:5:5) foll alt rows. Work 1 row. Cast off rem 12(15:14:18) sts.

With right side facing, rejoin yarn to rem sts and complete to match first side.

NECK AND HOOD EDGING

Fold hood in half and join top seam. With 3¾mm (No 9/US 4) circular needle and right side facing, k up 32(34:38:42) sts along right front edge of opening to shoulder, 69(73:75:77) along hood edge to top seam, 69(73:75:77) sts along hood edge to base and 32(34:38:42) sts along left front edge of opening to base. 202(214:226:238) sts. Work backwards and forwards in rows. Work 25(27:29:31) rows in rib as given for Sleeves. Cast off loosely in rib.

TO MAKE UP

Lap right side of front and hood edging over left and sew to base of front opening. Sew on sleeves, placing centre of sleeves to shoulder seams. Beginning at top of welts, join side seams, then sleeve seams, reversing seams half way on cuffs. Turn back cuffs.

ROWAN YARN ADDRESSES

Rowan Yarns are widely available in yarn shops. For details of stockists and mail order sources of Rowan Yarns, please write or contact the distibutors listed below.

UNITED KINGDOM
Rowan Yarns
Green Lane Mill
Holmfirth
West Yorkshire HD7 1RW
Tel: (01484) 681 881

USA
Westminster Fibres
5 Northern Boulevard
Amherst
NH 03031
Tel: (603) 886 5041/5043

AUSTRALIA
Coats Spencer Crafts
Level 1
382 Wellington Road
Private Bag 15
Mulgrave North
Victoria 3170
Tel: (39) 561 2288

BELGIUM
Pavan
Koningin Astridlaan 78
B9000 Gent
Tel: (092) 21 85 94

CANADA
Diamond Yarn
9697 St. Laurent
Montreal
Quebec H3L 2N1
Tel: (514) 388 6188

Martin Ross
Unit 3
Toronto
Ontario M3J 2L9
Tel: (416) 736 6111

DENMARK
Ruzicka
Hydesbyvej 27
DK 4990 Saskoing
Tel: (8) 54 70 78 04

FRANCE
Elle Tricote
52 rue Principale
67300 Schiltigheim
Tel: (33) 88 62 65 31

GERMANY
Wolle + Design
Wolfshover Strasse 76
52428 Julich Stetternich
Tel: (49) 2461 54735

HOLLAND
de Afstap
Oude Leliestraat 12
1015 Amsterdam
Tel: (020) 623 1445

HONG KONG
East Unity Company Ltd
RM 902
Block A
Kailey Industrial Centre
12 Fung Yip Street
Chai Wan
Tel: (852) 2869 7110

ICELAND
Stockurinn
Kjorgardi
Laugavegi 59
ICE-101 Reykjavik
Tel: (01) 551 82 58

ITALY
Victoriana
Via Fratelli Pioli 14
Rivoli
Torino
Tel: (011) 95 32 142

JAPAN
Diakeito Co Ltd
2-3-11 Senba-Higashi
Minoh City
Osaka 562
Tel: (0727) 27 6604

NORWAY
c/o Ruzicka
(see Denmark)

SWEDEN
Wincent
Norrtulsgaten 65
11345 Stockholm
Tel: (08) 673 70 60

Yarn, kits, ready-to-wear garments, books and toys are available from Debbie Bliss's shop:

Debbie Bliss
365 St. John Street
London EC1V 4LB
Tel: (0171) 833 8255
Fax (0171) 833 3588
e-mail: www.debbiebliss.freeserve.co.uk.

ACKNOWLEDGEMENTS

This book would not have been possible without the invaluable contribution of the following people:

The knitters: Pat Church, Connie Critchell, Shirley Kennet, Maisie Lawrence, Beryl Salter, and Frances Wallace.

Penny Hill, who helped organise the knitters, and me!

The children: a big thank you to Adam, Billy, Ciara, Charlotte, Cameron, Chloe, Edie, Ellie, Ella, Felix, Isabella, James, Katherine, Mali, Max, Olivia, Paige, Sam, Sasha, Thea, and of course, the dad of Sam and Max, Hans.

Tina Egleton, who checked all the patterns.

Sandra Lousada, who not only created the beautiful photographs but as usual committed herself totally to the project.

Christine Knox, who went to great lengths to reflect the style of the knits with the perfect accessories.

Heather Jeeves, my wonderful agent.

Denise Bates, my editor, who initiated the project and showed such enthusiasm for it.

The publishers would like to thank the following for lending clothes and props for photography:

fig. (01728 660551)
Membery's (0181 876 2910)
Rachel Riley (0171 259 5969)
Start-rite (01603 423841)